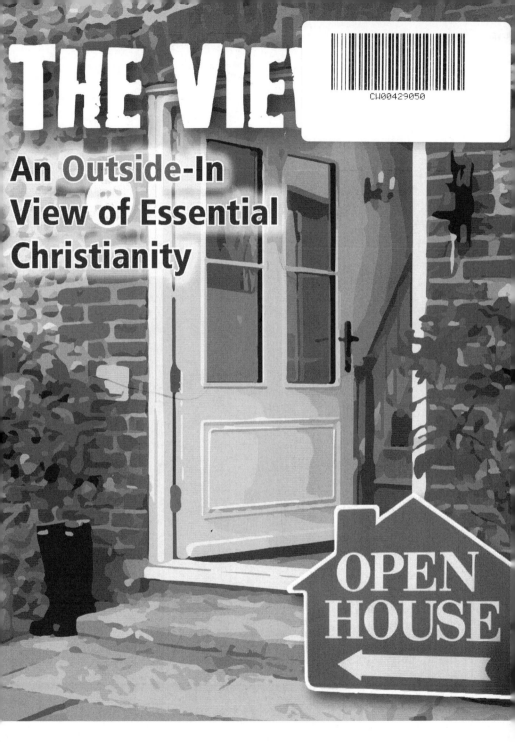

THE VIE

An Outside-In View of Essential Christianity

OPEN HOUSE

OHN R BALDOCK

DayOne

@ John R. Baldock 2019

ISBN 978-1-84625-635-6

British Library Cataloguing in Publication Data available.

All Scripture quotations unless stated otherwise, are from
The New International Version (2011).
Other Bible references are The Living Bible (1971).
Used by permission. All rights reserved.

Published by Day One Publications
Ryelands Road, Leominster, HR6 8NZ
Telephone 01568 613 740 Fax 01568 611 473
North America Toll Free 888 329 6630
email—sale@dayone.co.uk
website—www.dayone.co.uk

Cover and internal design by Kathryn Chedgzoy (k-c-design.co.uk)
Printed by 4edge Limited

THE VIEWING

An Outside-In View of
Essential Christianity

Introduction

The Viewing addresses 70 questions that are often raised by people who don't consider themselves to be Christians, who may even be unsure if they believe that God exists. Many of these are also asked by Christians; thoughtful people who have unresolved queries. Maybe you have considered some of these questions and would really like to find answers that satisfy you. As you read you won't come across forceful, cleverly constructed arguments designed to prove a point. *The Viewing* provides honest, straightforward explanations, the sort that you might hope would be shared during a relaxed conversation.

House viewers need to see past the current decor and furnishing, imagining how the different room spaces might work for them; this book requires no such translation. *The Viewing* doesn't use religious language and isn't about religious practices – it reveals the essence of Christian faith, based entirely on what can be understood from what the Bible has to show us.

We are all used to books being organised in chapter format, but this one has a twist – the questions are grouped around the features of a house. You are invited to journey through this building, checking out the structure and each of the rooms.

When viewing a house you may be more interested in certain aspects than in others, perhaps the kitchen, lounge or garden. *The Viewing* is designed to support selective reading; however, there are some topics that it is best not to miss out. These are prefixed ❖ within the table of Contents.

When you complete your viewing it is decision time - is this the house for you?

Viewing Particulars

THE FOUNDATIONS

Just as the foundations are the starting point for a house, we start with some fundamental topics that define the context for everything that follows.

THE ROOMS

The Study

This is the place for deep thought; it holds questions about our understanding of God and the Bible.

The Lounge

This is the primary social room; it holds questions about interaction with other people, including people of other religious beliefs.

The Television Room

Television gives us a window into places, experiences and situations that are not part of our everyday lives; this room holds questions about topics that could be classed as 'other worldly', such as heaven.

The Kitchen

This is the most technical room in a house; it holds questions related to religious rules and practices.

The Dining Room

This tends to be a formal room, where meals are enjoyed in company, and conversations occur; this room holds questions related to the church.

The Bathroom

This is the place where bodily waste is disposed of, and bodies are cleansed; this room holds questions related to guilt, forgiveness and spiritual health.

The Bedroom

This is the room where sexual interaction normally occurs; it holds questions related to sexual intimacy and relationships.

THE ROOF

This protects the house and occupants from the elements - rain, wind, cold or the rays of the sun. The roof contains questions about suffering.

THE GARDEN

Unlike the inside of the house, an accompanying garden is directly impacted by environmental and seasonal changes. This section holds questions related to changes that we experience in the world, about the prospects for change in our individual lives, and about responsibility for our environment.

THE CONTRACT

This last section holds questions related to completing the Contract. That is, moving from the world of scepticism and enquiry into a place of commitment to, and relationship with, God.

THE FOUNDATIONS

❖ Question 1 – What is a Christian?

Where to Start

The story is told of someone who, when driving in Ireland, stopped to ask a local resident for directions; the response was along the lines of: "if I was going to that place then I wouldn't start from here." Wherever you, the reader, are starting from in terms of belief in God, the fact that you are reading this book indicates that you are hoping to understand some things that you are confused or unsure about in relation to the Christian faith. We need to begin somewhere, and perhaps the best approach is to 'dive in at the deep end' and start by considering the fundamental question 'What is a Christian?'.

The term 'Christian' can be used to mean different things, depending on who you speak to. This creates uncertainty as to what genuine Christianity looks like, and confusion about what makes a person a Christian.

Recognising the Real McCoy

Whilst we may reasonably look to the effect in a person's life as a guide to the validity of whatever faith they profess, for this to reflect Christian faith there has to actually be faith there in the first place. So, 'doing good' does not make someone Christian, although being a Christian can be expected to result in doing good. The fact that someone may support a charity named 'Christian xxx' doesn't make them a Christian. Neither does the name of the charity, nor the work that it does, make it Christian; it is only if its foundations and ongoing motivation are based in God and his leading that it will be a genuine reflection of Christianity.

Another area that needs clarification is the terminology of 'religion' and 'faith'. These terms are sometimes used interchangeably and can each be interpreted differently according to your standpoint. It has been said that a religious person is someone who seeks God. We were created with a tendency to do just that – to seek God. Religion is a global, historic

15

phenomenon; since the earliest times people in every part of the world have sought for meaning for their existence, and for an explanation for their circumstances. In many ways this is a good thing, and religious followers are usually 'good' people. However, religious observance does not in itself point to genuine faith. As this topic is focussed on the question "What is a Christian?" we will leave aside considerations of non-Christian religion for the time being, but will pick this up later in the 'Lounge' section of the book.

What is Faith?

If religion is defined as a seeking after God, what is faith? Fundamental to faith is the placing of reliance upon God, based on relationship. Because faith requires reliance, it is practical; it has to actually cause change in us.[1]

The biggest airliner in the world, the Airbus A380, is rated to a maximum take-off weight of 575 metric tonnes; this is an impressive machine. In July 2011 my wife Jean and I were privileged to travel to Australia on the A380, to witness our son's wedding. It is almost incredible that such a huge and heavy craft should be capable of taking off from the ground and travelling through the sky for such long distances, but it does. It is one thing to imagine it, or even to witness the take-off and landing; but it requires faith to actually travel on it (and to sleep during the process). Why did we do it? Because we knew that this huge machine had successfully made the same journey many times previously, and we knew that many tens of thousands of people had safely travelled this way before us. Apart from this tangible evidence, we were also confident because of the excellent reputation of the plane builders and operators.

So it is with Christian faith. For me to acknowledge God's marvellous characteristics, to appreciate what he has done for me and the fact that he loves me, is all good, but it is only when I entrust myself to him, based on what I know about him, that I exercise faith. Faith is more than 'hope'. Many people hope that they will win the lottery, but that is actually wishful thinking; it isn't faith because there isn't a realistic expectation, but only a very remote chance, of being successful. Faith is different; faith is based on certain conviction.

The Basis for Faith

Let's consider the basis for belief that someone needs to be convinced of in order to become a Christian. This is summarised in the following five points:

- Belief in the existence of God – who is the creator and sustainer of the universe.[2]

- Belief in Jesus the Son of God – that he was born and lived a life in total obedience to God.[3]

- Recognition of personal failure to live the way that is pleasing to God.[4]

- Belief that Jesus died on the cross and, by doing so, took upon himself the consequences of our wrongdoing, guilt and shame.[5]

- Recognition that God offers forgiveness and a new life to anyone who asks to be reconciled to him, based on the work done by Jesus when he died in our place.[6]

To become a Christian (Christ Person) we need to recognise the truth of these and then, on this basis, to ask God for forgiveness for the wrong that we have done, and ask for the reconciliation that he offers. This is an entirely personal thing. Although other people may explain, may encourage, and may even pray with you, it is only through individual conviction of these truths that any spiritual change can occur. Words alone make no difference; they have to be accompanied by faith (conviction of truth)[7].

This outlines very simply what makes a person a Christian; but this explanation itself may well have raised questions in your mind. As indicated earlier, we needed to start somewhere; we will look in detail at all of these ideas, and many more, under later topics.

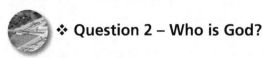

❖ Question 2 – Who is God?

Setting the Scene

As humans we have an instinct to try to understand who we are and where we belong; we have a need to find purpose. This has resulted in a diverse range of religious thought and practice, and a variety of ideas about a higher being. Accordingly, any consideration of Christianity has to begin with an understanding of who God is. The Greeks created a pantheon of 'gods', whereas some primitive religions are based on 'local' deities. Then there are of course those religions that recognise only one divine being. Included within these is Christianity.[1] We will consider other religions later, but for now we are concerned with the Christian understanding of who God is. The question 'who is God?' brings us back to the first of the statements shown within the previous topic, where we defined God as the 'creator and sustainer of the universe'. It is fair to say that this is the highest possible definition that we could have; when we speak of God we understand him as the one who brought into being everything that we can be aware of – absolutely everything.

Into Perspective

In mankind's infancy, the world itself seemed unthinkably large and mysterious, not to mention the heavenly bodies that could be discerned with the naked eye. Recently my wife and I visited Hereford and took the opportunity to see the Map of Mundi that is housed in the cathedral there. At first glance this ancient artefact looks to be a dull and uninspiring archaism; it is only when its 'story' is explained that one can start to appreciate its significance. This map was drawn on a single calf skin in the year 1300, and aims to depict the entire world that was known at that time; a world that was unaware of the existence of either the Americas or Australasia. Today our knowledge of our world and our awareness of the cosmos are much greater than in the year 1300. We now understand that our local solar system is a mere speck in the vastness of space. This magnified awareness does not change our understanding of God as the creator of everything; it serves only to magnify our appreciation of who God is.

Who Created God?

If we recognise that God is not a component of the cosmos but is the creator of everything, and therefore exists outside of the created order, then we still need to address the question 'who created God?' When my daughter was three years old we were in the habit of having bedtime chats; it is amazing what thoughts go through such young heads. One of her questions was just this one, 'Who made God?' I explained in a simple way that when God created everything, this wasn't just the physical universe itself, but also the laws by which it functions. I explained that the principle of 'cause and effect' is itself part of what God created. By this understanding, the question of who created God is a nonsense - the bottom line is quite simply that 'God is'. Interestingly, this is exactly what we learn about God from the Bible; when Moses asked God what name he was to be called by, the answer was "I Am".[2]

I appreciate that this may appear to be a clever ploy to evade the implicit question 'where did God come from?', but this leads us to a foundational point in understanding. We seek to understand God based on our own worldview – our own perspective. But by his very nature God is not constrained by this worldview.

The Goldfish Bowl

When our children were young, we kept some goldfish in a traditional round goldfish bowl. At different times we would look into the bowl and see what they were doing. Daily one of us would scatter some food on the surface of the water, which the fish would immediately come to eat. Periodically the fish bowl would be cleaned out. This cleaning entailed decanting the fish into a separate container, emptying the water, rinsing the gravel that sat on the bottom of the bowl and then refilling. The fish were then returned to their home, somewhat traumatised we imagined. We recognised that for the fish their existence was based on that goldfish bowl. They could probably see out just as we could look in, but their appreciation of what they would have seen would be severely constrained. At best they would have had some sort of awareness of the room in which their bowl normally sat, and of the kitchen where the cleanout occurred.

But they would not have had the slightest understanding of our life as a family, of what the children did when they disappeared wearing their school uniforms. This is not to mention the idea of my driving off to work to earn a living, or of the skills that I employed to do so. They would have no understanding of the sophistication of our language, the geography of the area where we lived, etc. To sum up, those fish were incapable of appreciating anything of the complexity of our human existence; they just lived in their bowl and peered out to see what they saw.

Our understanding of God is that he is the supreme being; he does not live in the 'goldfish bowl' that constrains our existence and understanding. Just as for the fish which did not have the slightest appreciation of the lives of my family, we as human beings cannot expect to fathom the depths of who God is. All we can do is to understand what is revealed about him. The letter to the Romans in the New Testament part of the Bible makes this very point stating: "... since the creation of the world God's invisible qualities – his eternal power and divine nature – have been clearly seen, being understood from what has been made..." [3]

God's Character

This brings us to another element of who God is, and this is to do with his character. He is the all-powerful being. But how does he behave, and how does he feel about us, mankind, the pinnacle of his creation? There are all sorts of things that can be asserted about God's character. Certainly, there is a wealth of evidence from the Bible telling us of his love, mercy, justice and faithfulness. But I want to employ a more fundamental indication of 'who' God is. I believe that we can discern a lot about the character of God from one essential aspect of what he created – beauty. Three things amaze me: firstly, that God made the whole of his creation so incredibly beautiful; secondly, that he made us with the senses and awareness to recognise and appreciate that beauty; and thirdly, that he gave us the ability to reflect his own creativity through fashioning beautiful things ourselves. It seems to me that God didn't need to create beauty; he just did it to enrich our lives and to bless us.

There is not one blade of grass, there is no colour in this world that is not intended to make us rejoice. **John Calvin**

The reality of the Creator God of Christianity blatantly reveals itself in His majestic handy-work. **R. Alan Woods**

❖ **Question 3 – How can I reconcile belief in God with reality?**

Asking the Right Question

This is a fundamental question, not so much because of the reference to God, but rather because of the idea of 'reality'. Perhaps another way to phrase this question would be to ask, "What is reality?"

If God is not real, or any of the things that are asserted in this book are not real, then it would be a complete nonsense to believe in them. There is an abundance of fiction to be read, such as Lewis Carroll's *Alice in Wonderland*, but these stories are just that, fiction, and no one in their right mind actually suggests that they represent reality or should be believed as factual.

Pick-and-Mix

Western culture is heavily practical, mathematical and pragmatic; on the surface we have little time for anything that cannot be explained or cannot be arrived at by calculation. But then, in contrast to this rationalistic worldview, we may also seek to nurture our 'spiritual side' by entertaining one or more of the cornucopia of 'spiritual' concepts that are available – new age mysticism, astrology, etc. Just about everything is thought to be valid with the proviso that we are each free to choose what we want to believe, like a 'pick and mix', based on our individual inclinations. In spite of this freedom to choose things that are not provable, there remains an obstacle to belief in the God of the Bible; not because this is 'other-worldly', but because we struggle to subscribe to the idea of the definite, the concept that there are 'right' and 'wrong' beliefs.

Using Blinkers

Sometimes a horse is fitted with blinkers – a pair of small leather screens attached to the bridle that prevent the horse from seeing sideways and behind – that are intended to protect it from being startled. It is as though we ourselves are choosing to wear blinkers so that we can see only what is immediately in front of us. And yet we still sense that there are other things, things to the side or behind, that we cannot see. This sense of the 'other' is stressful to the rationalistic mindset. We look to remove this stress by denying the existence of the God who is there. Instead we accommodate our 'spiritual side' by seeking for truth and 'reality' in various forms of alternate spirituality, anything that we imagine that the blinkers might be obscuring. The point is that whilst belief in God is indeed 'other worldly', what we can discover about him is just as real as the tangible everyday things that we experience through our five senses. God may be outside of our everyday experience, but he is no less real for that.

We may fear that we could be startled if we take off our spiritual blinkers, but isn't it worth the risk? My experience is that God is not in the business of frightening us; he will, however, amaze us with who he is, his love for us and what he has done for us.

Performing a Rationality Check

If you struggle to believe in God, then I want to suggest that you consider doing a rationality check on yourself. Think about what you do believe and act upon and see if there is anything that you allow into your life that isn't rational. For example, are you at all superstitious, do you ever read horoscopes, what are your feelings about death, dead people and the possibility of an existence after death? There are so many things that can creep into our worldview that are not rational, and yet something that is actually very sensible and rational, the existence of the Creator God, we choose to view as 'unreal'. Admittedly, discovering 'facts' about God is somehow academic, but this book isn't about convincing people about facts. It is about introducing the possibility of a very real and experiential relationship with God who created us and who has a purpose for our lives.[1]

❖ Question 4 – What is the Bible?

Changing the Question

Most people know what the Bible is, or at least imagine that they do. Originally the question for this topic was 'Why would I believe the Bible?', but it became obvious that there is a need first of all to explain what the Bible actually is. Understanding what the Bible is has to come before anyone can think about believing what the Bible says.

Before we look at what the Bible contains, let me explain what Christians believe the Bible to be. It is often referred to as the 'word of God', recognising that the purpose of the Bible is to help us to understand something of God's heart for mankind. Taken as a whole, it is his message to us. Now there are some who take a rather literal view on this, effectively seeing the text of the Bible as something that was directly dictated by God. To my mind this view of the Bible text doesn't take proper account of the human contribution. Christians believe that the Bible was inspired by God, the truth of the message it contains being preserved by God over a long period of time. However, most people recognise that men had a very real role and responsibility in recording what the Bible actually tells us. It is the truth contained within the Bible that has spiritual power, rather than the specific words themselves. This is not to suggest that the Bible is devoid of anything that can be taken as having come directly from God. There clearly are many passages that give us the actual words God has spoken; for instance, the words spoken over Jesus at his baptism, as recorded in the Gospel according to Matthew: "And a voice from heaven said, 'This is my Son, whom I love; with him I am well pleased.'" [1]

Into the Library

Having seen something of why the Bible is held so highly by Christians, we now come to look at what it actually is in literature terms. Some years ago my sister-in-law, Anita, surprised us greatly when she told us that she had started going to church; prior to this she had shown no interest in God whatsoever. After a while Anita asked us to buy her a Bible; she had visited a bookshop expecting to make a simple request for a Bible, but was thwarted by questions about which version etc. Anita was totally confused by this and so asked for our help; she seemed pleased with the Bible we bought for her and was enjoying reading it. However, sometime later when I again asked how she was getting on, she told me that she wasn't reading it anymore. I asked her where she had started reading, only to be told, not unreasonably, that she started "at the beginning of course."

The point is that the Bible is actually not a book, albeit that it appears as a single volume on the bookshelf. The word 'Bible' originates from the Greek word 'biblios', which actually refers to a 'library'. The Bible is a library of 66 separate 'books' and letters, that have been brought together. These were written and compiled over a very long period of time, and contain different types of literature: historical, poetic, biographical, etc.

My sister-in-law had ploughed into the first books of the Bible but ground to a halt in the third of these, the book known as Leviticus. Leviticus is a challenging book for anyone as it goes into considerable detail about all of the rules for living that the Jews tried to follow in the days before Jesus. There are lots of more interesting and easier-to-appreciate books in the Bible; most people would place Leviticus near the bottom of their list of reading priorities.

The Catalogue

The Bible is divided into two sub-libraries, called Testaments. The 'Old Testament' relates to the time before Jesus was born, starting with the creation of the universe, and the first man and woman (Adam and Eve). The 'New Testament' contains books that were written about Jesus and about the early days of the Christian church. The Bible story is continuous both historically and also in the message that it gives us about God's relationship with mankind. The Old Testament promises the Jewish nation that a deliverer (or 'Messiah'), will come; the New Testament tells us how the deliverer promised in the Old Testament actually came, and explains the implications of his coming – the promised deliverer is Jesus.[2]

There are 66 books and letters in the Bible. The constituent components have been constant since they were formally agreed by councils of the

Christian church some 1600 years ago. Previous to that, whilst there was a broad common understanding of which books and letters were valid, there were many questionable writings in circulation. In the early days of the Christian church, as remains the case today, there were people pushing false ideas that undermined sound Christian teaching. Accordingly, some writings were excluded from the official collection of the Bible because of error in content or because they were deceitfully attributed to a respected writer, when there was solid evidence that they were not written by that person.

Getting to Where we are Now

Having thought briefly about how we got to the books that the Bible contains, we need also to consider the actual text of these books. Today we have numerous 'translations' of the Bible, in a huge number of languages. There are a great many English language versions, most of which have been produced over the last fifty years or so. Bible translation is based on the best available scholarship at the time that the translation work is undertaken, and on the best available original texts. Fragments of ancient Bible texts continue to be discovered. So, there are subtle changes between translations.

In addition to variations due to scholastic development, different 'translations' utilise different approaches in how the words are presented. Those who are familiar with the French language understand that the grammatical order of words in French differs to that of English. So it is with the original languages of the Bible. Translators need not only to use the most accurate words to translate the original, but to place these in the appropriate order for the language into which they are translating. Some modern Bible versions don't even aim for a word-for-word representation of the original language but concentrate rather on expressing the meaning of the original text. In this case, the specific words used are treated as of secondary importance; such versions are referred to as 'transliterations' rather than translations. A transliteration can be very helpful in providing a meaningful understanding of a particular passage, especially for someone who is new to reading the Bible.

What to Believe

From an early age I enjoyed the Bible and found it pleasurable to read – perhaps because I had a 'religious' inclination. However, after committing my life to God at the age of seventeen, one of my first decisions was that I would not believe anything simply because it was stated in the Bible. I appreciate that this was rather arrogant of me (I was seventeen!). However, I have actually never regretted taking this stance because it was based on the premise that Christian belief has to stand up to reasoned thought, and to be consistent. And so, in my early years as a Christian I needed to feel that I understood how things fitted together before including them in my personal belief system. After some time I discovered that, once subjected to scrutiny, everything that I came across in the Bible proved to be valid. As a result, my position changed to one where, in principle, I believe what I read, even if I don't yet understand it (or maybe don't like it).

Who is Pauline?

Some people have issues that undermine their confidence in the Bible text. When I had been a Christian for only a short time, I was asked by someone who I was working with if I accepted the 'Pauline' teaching in the Bible. I was at a loss as to what they were talking about – my first question was, "Who is Pauline?" I soon learned that some people effectively opt out of certain things that the Bible teaches, in this particular case some of the teachings found in the letters written by the apostle Paul (hence 'Pauline'). I am not going to take us into detail about all of the things that are sometimes raised to justify taking what the Bible says with a pinch of salt. I simply want to emphasise my own experience that the Bible in its entirety makes sense. The Bible, taken as a whole, enables us to gain a comprehensive and consistent understanding of God's purposes; there is no justification for discarding or discounting any part of it. This takes us back to the premise that the Bible is the 'word of God'; it is his message to mankind.[3] If this is the case, then there can be no scope for me to select which parts of it I will, and will not, accept.

❖ **Question 5 – If truth exists, how can I recognise it?**

What is Truth?

The one-time Roman Governor of Palestine, Pontius Pilate, is famously known for the rhetorical question that he addressed to Jesus: "What is truth?"[1] If this was a valid question 2000 years ago, it is even more so now. Why more so? – because the way that we think has changed. Whilst we are rationalistic in our thinking – we use reason as the basis of our decisions – at the same time we have jettisoned the idea of the 'definite'. We see this at even so fundamental a level as gender; some try to tell us that we no longer need to be bound by the way our bodies are formed in the womb.

Truth as a concept is very much out of vogue, because we no longer want to be constrained by the 'definite'; we want to be open to every possibility, every opinion, every option.

Communicating Truth

Admittedly there are circumstances where facts need to be seen in context to arrive at truth, where they can't simply be taken at face value, even though they are true facts. It is a long time since I have applied for a job, but I have always aimed to keep my CV up to date and ready for use. Some people exaggerate their achievements in order to gain an advantage. This is something that I would not consider doing, but I have found myself needing to do some 'interpretation'. I didn't go to university or study for a degree, but I did study for three years to gain a Bible College Diploma, and this study is listed on my CV; for most employers the thing that this will tell them is that I am 'very religious'. This is unfortunate not only because it is an untrue conclusion, but also because it fails to highlight the value of this training. To a Christian employer, Bible College training is totally understood and is appreciated; to a secular employer it is likely to create a negative impression. In fact at one job interview in the early years after I completed my course, I was asked outright whether I had lost my faith or just wanted the job as a stop-gap until work in the Christian sphere opened up to me. I subsequently amended my CV to identify this study at Bible College as 'theological and communication studies', in the hope that this tells people that I have a good brain and am a capable communicator. By the way, I said that I am not 'very religious'; you might wonder at this assertion, but it is the truth. Please refer to the topic in the Lounge section – Q16: 'What is the difference between religious observance and Christian faith?'

Handling the Grey

Truth can be tricky because life isn't always as black and white as we would like it to be. That doesn't mean that there is no such thing as truth; neither does it mean that we cannot know what is true. It may not always be possible to prove empirically what is and what is not true, but it is possible to become personally convinced of where the truth lies. I don't want to be overly subjective about this. What I am saying is that once all arguments have been considered, it is down to each individual to decide whether they acknowledge a thing as being true or not. To quote my wife, Jean, "Truth is what is left when lies are gone."

The idea of truth, and knowing what is true, is certainly a concept that is embraced within the Bible, specifically in Jesus' statement that is recorded in the Gospel according to John, "... you will know the truth, and the truth will set you free."[2] Bear in mind though that this was said to people who had become convinced about Jesus, and who acknowledged the rightness of what he was telling them about God.

Starting from Scratch

Today, sadly, we have lost those things that in the past were viewed as definite, true and constant. We question authority, we do not always feel bound to obey rules and we no longer automatically accept the Bible as truth, or even as relevant and worth becoming familiar with. Many years ago we lived in East Anglia, not very far from one of the big American air force bases that are located there. We made friends with Bob and Judy, whose home was just around the corner from us; at the time Bob was a US air force pilot. We discovered from Judy the concept of 'scratch baking'. Actually what we discovered was the term 'scratch', and that this is what the Americans call what we actually did all of the time – baking from a recipe using individual ingredients. The alternative to 'scratch' baking, we learned, was to use packet mixes where many of the ingredients are already provided in the correct proportions. It turned out that our American friends normally used packet mixes, because it was easier and more reliable than sourcing and measuring the ingredients for themselves.

Getting back to the idea of Truth, most people no longer enjoy the certainty of 'packet mixes', those things that used to be relied upon as definite and true, such as authorities, rules and the Bible. Instead everything has to be worked out and arrived at from scratch. As far as Christian faith is concerned it could be argued that this is no bad thing; it is preferable that someone believes what they have become personally convinced of, rather than acquiescing to some commonly held set of beliefs.

This still leaves us with the original question about recognising truth, and the answer has to be that we need to follow the scientific principle. We can arrive at truth by observing the evidence, considering the possible ways that this makes sense, and putting any resulting hypothesis to the test. This takes a degree of commitment, but it is a way to arrive at truth, and it is what this book is all about. If we face the facts, review the hypothesis and test the answers then we can expect to arrive at truth.

Knowing

Sometimes I am asked, "How can I know that these things about God are true?" And I always give the same answer – ask him. If you sincerely want to know if God is real, then ask him to convince you.[3] You don't have anything at all to lose – if he doesn't exist then you will soon know, and it will cost you nothing. But if he does exist, and if the message of the Bible is actually true, then you need to know for yourself so that you can decide what your response to him will be. Becoming convinced is a game changer. The question mark over God is transferred to us – the question changes to 'what am I going to do about it?' Now that I 'know', will I accept him or reject him? So, before progressing any further in this book, why not stop and ask God to show you what is true – "God, if you are there, please reveal truth to me so that I can know you for myself". (See the TV Room – Q 32: 'How can we know what God is saying to us?')

The Study

Question 6 – Isn't the Bible just a collection of myths and hearsay?

Fact or Fiction?

There are reasons why we might think that the Bible contains 'myths'. The first is if we decide to discount the miracles. The Bible is packed with what we may think of as miraculous events, whether particular events such as the healing miracles that Jesus performed, or stories of how individual people had some form of direct experience of God, such as when God spoke to Moses from a burning bush.[1] If we do not accept that the miraculous can occur, then we will certainly see the Bible as a mythical document. However, if this were the case then the Bible would be useless to us even as a basis for moral teaching, because it would be full of lies and deceit and therefore could not be seen as a sound foundation for moral truth.

Truth in Isolation

Traditionally, one of the main ways that the Christian church has taught people is through the stories that are contained within the Bible. This isn't a bad thing in itself as it makes the content of the Bible accessible, especially where the audience is illiterate as has generally been the case throughout much of the history of the church. There can, however, be a problem with teaching using stories if they are not given in the overall context of the purposes of God. That is to say, if individual stories are taught in isolation – the well-known story of Noah and the Ark, for example.[2] When the Bible is viewed holistically it isn't the stories that are the main message but God's purposes for mankind; the stories serve to illustrate and reinforce that main message.

Unbelievable?

Some people accept the miraculous to an extent but choose not to trust certain Bible stories because they view them as unbelievable. This is an understandable position as there are things recorded in the Bible that at first glance appear not to be credible. An example is the story of Jonah being swallowed by a large fish (or whale) and later being regurgitated alive so that he can fulfil the task that God had given him to do.[3] If we look at the Bible as a purely literary document then it is reasonable to discount something like the story of Jonah, if we consider this incredible. On the other hand, if we understand the Bible to be the 'Word of God' then it is difficult to justify picking and choosing which parts we are going to accept. If the Bible is a purely human creation, then we can treat it as such; the moment that we recognise that God has a 'hand in it' then we have to see it in totality as being reliable and trustworthy.

Does this mean that there can be no inconsistencies? No, it doesn't. What it does mean is that there can be nothing that is seriously misleading – remember that man has been involved as well as God, and man can make errors. The need for the Bible to be 'sound' is why it was so important for the Christian leaders in the early centuries of the church to define what books and letters were included within the Bible and what were excluded.

Inconsistencies

If the Bible is the 'Word of God' then we have to conclude that it does not contain false content; everything that it says happened, did happen. There may have been slight inaccuracies in recording, some apparent inconsistencies. Where these occur, rather than being seen negatively, they are often cited as evidence for the overall reliability of the Bible. If the Bible were a fabrication, an elaborate ruse, then any obvious inconsistencies would have been removed or avoided. The fact that they remain indicates that the original writers were doing their utmost to record things accurately, as they were remembered, and that subsequent copyists were conscientious in accurately transposing what they were copying without making 'corrections'.

Question 7 – Does modern science contradict the Bible?

An Honest Mistake

In the year 1560 Bishop James Usher of Armagh, in Ireland, published a work in which he famously calculated that the earth was formed at midday on October 23rd in the year 4004 BC. To most people today this conjecture is likely to bring a smile, but at the time it was an entirely honest and scholarly effort to understand when the earth was formed. The good bishop used the information contained in the Old Testament part of the Bible as the basis for his calculation. The problem was that he used the record in the Bible as though it was technically precise. This is not to suggest that the Bible record is in any respect wrong, or even knowingly misleading; simply that Bishop Usher took it to be what it was not, coming to a technical conclusion based on non-technical data. The bishop's approach is perfectly reasonable to a modern mind, based on the assumption that when the Bible gives us a genealogical string, the generations are contiguous. But this is not how some of the recorded genealogies were meant to be understood. It would be as though we were to look at the female monarchs in the British Royal family, stating that Elizabeth II followed Victoria, who followed Elizabeth I. This is perfectly correct, but also capable of being misconstrued. We would 'lose' a great deal of history were we to imagine that there were no intervening monarchs. In the case of the biblical record, our modern understanding is at odds with that of the original writers, who would not have envisaged how their recorded facts might be used.

Seeds of Dissention

Unfortunately, Bishop Usher's conclusion set the church establishment at odds with the conclusions of the men of science – a rift that was so unnecessary. However, for many people the date of the formation of the earth is a rather smaller matter than an issue that came about with the serious scientific work of Charles Darwin, and his theory of evolution. There are three points to be made in connection with this.

Firstly, that it is perfectly reasonable to hold onto both biblical truth and scientific fact, without there being a conflict between them.

Secondly, that although today there is a tendency to teach the theory of evolution as if it were fact, the idea that mankind evolved from apes, and originated from single cell organisms, is an unproven theory.

Thirdly, that for the atheist who is adamant that there is no God, there is no alternative to believing that evolutionary theory is actually fact.

The God of Order

As a teenager I was drawn much more to science subjects than humanities or arts, although I was to make a pitiable effort at physics and chemistry 'A' level exams. However, my study of these subjects did teach me about the scientific method, and I still have an interest in science. At the beginning of the Bible, in the first chapter of the book of Genesis, we read that God formed man and woman; we are also told that they were commissioned to subdue the earth:

> God blessed them and said to them, 'Be fruitful and increase in number; fill the earth and subdue it. Rule over the fish in the sea and the birds in the sky and over every living creature that moves on the ground.[1]

We can understand from this that God's commissioning of mankind is intended to encompass both exploration and scientific research, such that we may come to understand the 'works of his hands'. Some people think of God as if he is a divine magician, who formed the creation in an arbitrary way, like an abstract artist throwing coloured paints on a canvas to see what patterns they create. This perception does not accord with the Bible, or the Christian experience of God; he is orderly, purposeful, and precise. God created in a way that permits our scientific investigation so that we are able to discover the mechanisms by which the world around us functions.

Origins of Life

Some years ago, my wife and I visited the world famous Kew botanical research gardens in west London. Amongst the towering glasshouses with their steamy tropical environments packed with sample species from across the globe, we discovered a representation of what the curators imagined the crucible of life to be like: a 'hot, muddy, rock pool of primordial soup'. This was of particular interest to me because I had just finished reading a scholarly book by two scientists, entitled *Origins of Life* in which they argued very convincingly that the statistical probabilities for the spontaneous formation of life on Earth make this effectively impossible.[2] I was bemused to find that Kew was still lending credence to this outdated theory.

However, it is even more interesting that, unwilling to recognise that divine intervention was needed for life to appear on Earth, atheists now assume that life must have been imported from another planet. Given the statistical improbability of spontaneous life, this may sound reasonable – if you are an atheist who discounts there being a creator God. Those who acknowledge God, and also recognise order in what he has created, have more options open to them. They are free to believe what are clearly proven, sound, scientific conclusions, whilst also recognising that everything is the work of our creator. Scientific discoveries demonstrate the complexity and wonder of God's creation.

There Would be a Problem if ...

We need also to look at what the Bible tells us in the first chapter of the first book, Genesis. It is here that we are given to understand the order in which the creation occurred. Genesis tells us what was created on each of six 'days', culminating with the creation of the first man and woman. It has only been as modern science has developed, that we have been confronted with evidence that appears to contradict what the Bible states.

If scientific discovery could demonstrate convincingly that the order of the creation depicted in the first chapter of Genesis was incorrect, then there would be a problem. However, this is not the case. We might reasonably conclude that the correlation of the order given in the Bible, and that now understood from following the scientific process, is a huge endorsement of biblical accuracy and itself points to divine revelation in the book of Genesis.

Something to Celebrate

We have looked at just a few areas where there is an apparent contradiction between the Bible and science. A holistic appreciation of the orderly creation, and recognition that this came about at the hand of God, leaves us with no contradiction. Rather, it enables us to celebrate his handiwork as we learn more about the mechanisms that he set in motion.

❖ Question 8 – Who is Jesus – is he for real?

Part 1: The Historical Jesus

Most people are aware of the name Jesus, or Christ, as a swear word if nothing else. Jesus is a historical figure who lived in the first part of the first century AD, during the Roman occupation of what was then known as Palestine – the land of the Jewish people.

The names Jesus and Christ are often linked together, a bit like a first name and surname, which is quite appropriate except that instead of 'Jesus Christ' we would be better to speak of 'Jesus the Christ'. This is because his name is Jesus, but Christ is his title, meaning 'Anointed One'.

Everyone was Waiting

Jesus was born into a Jewish family without status, wealth or power. But there were a few things that marked out this infant as very different to others, for instance that he was expected. Mothers normally 'expect' their babies, but Jesus was also expected in a more profound way – his arrival had been anticipated for hundreds of years, and by the whole Jewish nation.[1] This obviously doesn't match the circumstances of his birth, but there lies the problem; the nation anticipated the coming of Jesus but proved incapable for the most part of recognising him when he arrived. If you are familiar with the Christmas story, then you will be aware of how Jesus came to be born. But if not, then suffice it to say that he was born to a young woman, a virgin, but he did not have a human father – Jesus was born the 'Son of God'.[2]

The Bottom Line

To many people this is a very strange story; not simply because Jesus' conception was miraculous but because it is not immediately clear why he had to be born as a human baby at all. This brings us to the crux of the question that we are examining – 'Who is Jesus?' The story of the Old Testament part of the Bible is one of disappointment, beginning right at the start with the first man and woman in the Garden of Eden. We see this disappointment crystallised in the Old Testament history books, especially the second book of Kings. This book gives a potted history of most of the kings of the Jewish nation over a period of 293 years. Against many of these kings we read that they 'did evil in the eyes of God'. It would be wrong to suppose that this failure to please God rested with the kings alone; it was endemic among the people generally. Yes, there were times when God was honoured, but such periods were soon followed by times of compromise and disobedience to God's laws. The bottom line was that for mankind to be able to be restored to God, he needed to step in and provide a way for this to happen; we were incapable of doing this for ourselves. We could be excused for thinking that the purpose of Jesus' coming was to teach God's ways, or to launch a movement, but that was not it. Jesus came to make a way for individuals to be reconciled to God, and he could only do this because he was a human being like us and he was the Son of God.

Historical Fact

You may think that this seems rather fanciful but be assured that Jesus is no myth. Apart from the Bible, the historicity of Jesus is documented by secular sources. For instance, the Roman historian Tacitus mentions in his 'Annals' that Jesus was executed by Pontius Pilate. Obviously, secular sources will only reference the historical events surrounding Jesus; they can't be expected to tell us about the significance of Jesus in the purposes of God – we can only understand about this by what the Bible tells us. Jesus' life is documented in four separate accounts in the beginning of the New Testament section of the Bible, in books known as the four gospels – we might assume that all four of these accounts were included in the Bible because the story of Jesus is foundational to Christian belief. Although these four accounts tell the same story, there are differences of emphasis, which serve to illustrate their independence, and point to their authenticity. If you would like to understand more about Jesus, then the last of these four accounts, the Gospel according to John, would be a good place to start.

Based on what the four gospel accounts record about what Jesus said and did, someone once came to the logical conclusion that Jesus must have been either mad, bad or God. If he is God then his story is not so very strange – but it is up to each of us to make up our own mind as to which we believe he was – God, or something else.

Part 2: What Jesus means for us

Other people may differ, but for me the most profound event in human history was when a young virgin, named Mary, became pregnant with Jesus.[3] Why was this event, which most Christians don't bother to mark with a day of celebration, of such significance? It is because through that one act God committed his Son to become a human being, to be irrevocably and permanently bound to humanity. The conception of Jesus as a human baby bound him to humanity not just for the short time of his life on earth, but for eternity – Jesus who now sits on a heavenly throne remains both God and Man.[4] This very fact points to what Jesus means for us. Jesus is God's rescue plan for mankind, providing the means to effect this rescue, but also showing God's heart for us. Jesus took his human nature into eternal union with his divine nature.

The Rift

When our children were growing up there were certain behaviours for which we, as parents, had zero tolerance. These included deliberate lying, deceit and disrespect for us. Our children were well aware of these boundaries and knew what the consequences would be if they transgressed them. We did not have rules so as to be harsh with our children, but to ensure that they would develop as honourable people; the rules were in place to bless our children. It wasn't wrong actions that we were determined to prevent, but wrong attitudes. God has boundaries; when we transgress these boundaries we cause a rift between us and God – it is this rift that Jesus came to repair. The Bible uses the term 'sin' to refer to heart attitudes that displease God and cause this rift.

The writer Paul states in his New Testament letter to the Romans:

> *You see, at just the right time, when we were still powerless, Christ died for the ungodly. Very rarely will anyone die for a righteous person, though for a good person someone might possibly dare to die. But God demonstrates his own love for us in this: while we were still sinners, Christ died for us.*[5]

Our reconciliation to God was made possible because Jesus paid the price for our wrongdoing. When he accepted the punishment that we justly deserve, he died in our place, being unjustly executed by the Roman authorities to please the rulers of the Jews. It is important to understand, however, that Christians do not rely on a dead Jesus for their reconciliation to God. The Bible account of these events tells us that following Jesus' death his body was laid in a tomb; on the third day God raised him back to life.[6] Jesus met with his followers on several occasions after this, culminating with his being taken up to heaven in front of their very eyes.[7]

❖ **Question 9 – What is meant by the 'Trinity' and is this important?**

Make or Break

In the Foundations section, under the question 'Who is God?', we saw that God is knowable, but only to a limited extent; God is so much more than we are, and more than we are capable of appreciating. It is helpful to bear this in mind now that we are looking at the Christian teaching about the Trinity, simply because we are very limited in our ability to understand the things of God. The Christian understanding is that God is one, but in three persons – God the Father, God the Son (Jesus), and God the Holy Spirit. The idea of the Trinity is implicit within the Bible, although the word 'trinity' is not mentioned specifically.

The Trinity is the foundational teaching of Christianity; without this there can be no Christianity.

The very idea of three persons existing as one is hard for us to appreciate, and ever since New Testament times there have been those who have promoted alternative, false, understandings of who God is. Wrong teachings about the nature of God can be summarised by three theological terms:

Tritheism   – this states that there are three Gods

Unitarianism   – this states that there is one God and that Jesus is NOT divine (not God)

Modalism   – this states that there is one God, like an actor playing three parts

The Christian teaching about God existing as 'Three in One' is known by the technical term 'Trinitarianism'.

Persistent Threat

In those early years following the time of Jesus, the church was confronted by a plethora of false teaching that was seriously flawed, and very dangerous. Consequently, there was an urgent need to agree a definition about

43

things such as the nature of God, particularly the relationship between the three persons to whom the Bible texts attribute the status of God. These definitions took the form of 'creeds' that were drafted and agreed during a number of church councils, where leaders from far and wide gathered to thrash out what was sound teaching and what was error. The best known of these is probably the 'Apostles' Creed', which some traditional churches recite regularly as part of their religious liturgy. The clearest statement of the church in respect of the teaching about the Trinity is found in the less well known 'Athanasian Creed'. This creed states, in precise and almost legal terminology:

> *.... we worship one God in trinity and the trinity in unity, neither blending their persons nor dividing their essence.*

> *For the person of the Father is a distinct person, the person of the Son is another, and that of the Holy Spirit still another.*

> *But the divinity of the Father, Son, and Holy Spirit is one, their glory equal, their majesty coeternal. What quality the Father has, the Son has, and the Holy Spirit has ....*

A Length of Rope

Because the Trinity is a difficult concept to get our heads around, various attempts have been made to find an analogy to aid our understanding, none of which are perfect. When I was preparing a series of talks on the Trinity, I asked God how I should illustrate this and felt that he showed me to use the analogy of a length of rope. Think about it – rope is normally made up of three strands; these strands have exactly the same characteristics, and they are held tightly together entirely by their own inclination to stay together. A length of rope always, and only, acts as one but we can clearly see that it has three distinct constituent parts. So it is with the three persons of the Trinity.

Essential Qualification

Why is the Trinity important for us? Because this teaching makes it clear that Jesus (the Son) is fully God. It is only because he is God that he is able to make a way for our reconciliation to God. If he was only a man then he would not have been qualified to do this. At best Jesus' own death could only be valid for the redemption of one other person. But because he is God and man, his death is able to be the basis for all of us to be reconciled to God. This is encapsulated by a statement in the second letter to the Corinthians, in the New Testament, which states:

> *For Christ's love compels us, because we are convinced that one died for all, and therefore all died.*[1]

We saw earlier that Trinity teaching is implicit but not explicit in the Bible, but there is no shortage of Bible texts that point very clearly to God being in Trinity. Here are just a few (with emphases added):

Describing how mankind came to be created –

> *Then God said, "Let **us** make mankind in **our** image, in **our** likeness ..."*[2]

Referring to Jesus –

> *For to us a child is born, to us a son is given, and the government will be on his shoulders. And he will be called Wonderful Counsellor, **Mighty God**, Everlasting Father, Prince of Peace.*[3]

> *And a voice came from heaven: "**You are my Son**, whom I love; with you I am well pleased."*[4]

> *In the beginning was the Word, and the Word was with God, and **the Word was God**.*[5]

> *No one has ever seen God, but the one and only Son, **who is himself God** and is in the closest relationship with the Father, has made him known.*[6]

There are also clear statements in the New Testament that confirm the Christian understanding that God is one (i.e. not multiple gods):

> *"The most important one [law]," answered Jesus, "is this: 'Hear, O Israel: the Lord our God, the Lord is one.'"* [7]

> *So then ... we know that ... 'There is no God but one.'* [8]

❖ **Question 10 – What is meant by orthodox Christian belief?**

Setting the Standard

The Chambers dictionary defines the word 'orthodox' as: "sound in doctrine; believing, or according to, the received or established doctrines or opinions." As has been stated under other topics, we tend these days to want to make up our own minds as to what we will believe and are hesitant to adopt a 'standard' position – we want to be able to choose for ourselves. Accordingly, the idea of an 'orthodox' set of beliefs doesn't sit comfortably with many people. None the less, it is important to appreciate what is meant by Christian orthodoxy, and why this is very important. Please note that we are not specifically referring here to the Eastern Orthodox branch of the Christian faith.

Getting it Together

Contrary to what many may expect to be the case, the Christian church is not an institution, and neither for that matter is it a building. The Christian church is a spiritual entity that is centred upon God. Most Christians would date its existence from the event recorded in the second chapter of the New Testament book of the 'Acts of the Apostles', namely the experience of the first Christians during the celebration of the Jewish feast of Pentecost. These first believers in Jesus experienced the empowering of the Holy Spirit, and under that empowering proclaimed the message about Jesus to the multitudes who were gathered to celebrate that feast. The outcome, we are told, was that some 3,000 people were convinced to become followers of Jesus that day and were joined together with the initial group. This was not a human endeavour; it was God's doing.

The message of Jesus continued to be proclaimed such that the numbers grew quickly; the message spread far and wide resulting in the geographical spread of the church also being widely extended. In the midst of this burgeoning, organic 'body' of people, there were those who, presumably hoping to make a name for themselves, distorted the message of the church and did what we have looked at earlier – they believed and taught whatever seemed right to them. The result was that there were a variety of teachings, or ideas, circulating that undermined the truth. This is evidenced in some of the letters contained within the New Testament; these letters make reference to 'false teachers'.[1]

In the midst of this melee of different ideas and teachings, the church needed to define precisely what accorded with the teaching of Jesus, who he was understood to be, and what was consistent with the things God was revealing generally, both through the Old Testament writings and also through those men whom Jesus had appointed to lead the church. This definition of sound doctrine is what is known as orthodox Christian belief and has stood in place since the early centuries of the Christian church. Central to this matter of orthodox belief is a right understanding of who Jesus is, which is why the doctrine of the Trinity is so crucial to Christian faith.

Repetition

Surprisingly, the church today still has to contend with many of the same false teachings that were extant in those early years of Christianity. There are a number of religious groups, or sects, that claim to be Christian or 'church', but who teach ideas that are not orthodox; for example, Jehovah's Witnesses, Mormons, 'Christian Science', and Unitarians. Within the scope of orthodox belief we still find many very divergent groups, but these all hold to the basic tenets of orthodox Christian teaching; these include Anglicans (Episcopalians), Methodists, Baptists and Pentecostals to name but a few. There are many things that are different amongst those that adhere to orthodox belief, significant and important differences, but on the key tenets of Christian teaching they stand on the same ground; their fundamental beliefs about the nature of God, and about who Jesus is, are orthodox.

Question 11 – Can God change?

All Change

I was employed for 20 years by a large multi-national IT Services Company. My wife says that the one thing that was permanent about my employer was change. Upheaval of one sort or another appeared to be seen by the company as positive. Whether positive or not, change is something that we have to accept in our lives generally. Change is a normal part of human experience. There are different stages of life, with different challenges and opportunities. Our environment also changes throughout each year, and to a lesser extent from one year to the next.

In addition to those changes that we have little, if any, control over, we are accustomed to internal changes – changing our minds about things. This might be a change of view resulting from study or education, or it might be a change of decision based on reconsideration. Some people are happy to commit to something one day but later recant and fail to follow through on their promise. And so it may seem reasonable to imagine that God might also be inclined to change, to react or reconsider based on some change of circumstance.

Above all of That

Under the topic 'Who is God?' in the Foundations section (Q 2), we referred to God as the 'creator of everything' and therefore as standing outside of the created order. An initial logical conclusion from this is that God is in total control of everything and not vulnerable to imposed changes in the way that we as human beings are. It is also logical to understand that God is all-knowing, not only in the present but also in the past and the future. If we accept this premise, then we must also recognise that there are no surprises for God. If he knows everything then his decisions and actions are based on this full knowledge, and therefore there is nothing that would make him change what he has determined; he has no reasons for re-planning or changing in any respect.

Theologians use the term 'immutable' to refer to the attribute of God that relates to change. Orthodox Christian theology states that God is immutable, unchanging.

Here are two very clear references to God and 'change' in the Old Testament section of the Bible:

> God is not human, that he should lie,
>   not a human being, that he should change his mind.
> Does he speak and then not act?
>   Does he promise and not fulfil?[1]

> He who is the Glory of Israel does not lie or change his mind; for he is not a human being, that he should change his mind.[2]

And so, if God does not change then what does this mean for us?

The Rules Haven't Changed

If God does not change, then the promises he has made in the Bible have not changed either. This applies to those things that we would see as positive, his promises of blessing, and also those that we might see as negative, such as warnings about the consequences of our wrong actions. Some people believe that mankind is becoming more sophisticated with time and correspondingly 'better'. The idea of 'better' is hugely subjective, but so is the conclusion that we are becoming better. Clearly, we rejoice in our growing knowledge and understanding of the physical universe, but this awareness does not equate to growth in moral understanding, and certainly not growth in the appreciation of spiritual truth. In fact, it is arguable that the opposite is the case. Is there a tendency to assume that growth in understanding in the one area means that we 'know better' in the others also? Surely this would be extremely arrogant, which in itself points to our having lost our bearings in the moral and spiritual spheres. In a similar way to how we have tried to judge God from our own perspective, so we try to challenge his laws with our own frail, limited and blinkered understanding.

A New Revolution

The industrial revolution that occurred in the eighteenth and nineteenth centuries is known for two things: a massive thrust of mechanisation that radically changed human industry; and a total lack of understanding of, and moral focus upon, the needs of the workers who serviced this industry. The industrial revolution is paralleled today by the scientific revolution; there has been a massive growth in scientific research, knowledge and understanding, to which everything has been made subservient. Just as the human component of the industrial process was forced into servitude to production, so moral norms and spiritual truth have been made subject to the god of science; that which cannot be scientifically measured is discarded, or at best cynically undermined.

Focussing back onto the question – can God change? – we have to recognise that it is contrary to God's nature to do so and that he remains the same. Just as God himself does not change, there is no basis for suggesting that his guidance to us is any different today than when the biblical books were penned some 2000+ years ago. What was wrong then is still wrong; the consequences then still pertain today – what God said still stands. God hasn't changed his mind.

Question 12 – Why does God want a relationship with us?

A Free Lunch

Another way of putting this question would be 'What's in it for God?' Framing the question in this way reflects our own experience of life, which is sometimes expressed in the assertion that 'there is no such thing as a free lunch'. It is true that we are complex beings and even when our selfish reasons for acting are not immediately apparent, we often have hidden motives that are self-serving. And so it is not surprising that we might think that the same applies to God.

A Relational God

We cannot answer this question fully, because we are not able to fully understand God. That said, there are two specific themes in the Bible that go a long way to addressing this topic. The first appears in the few words in the beginning of the book of Genesis that we looked at when considering the question 'What is meant by the Trinity?' (Q 9): 'Then God said, "Let us make mankind in our image, in our likeness." The use of 'our' here highlights the plural nature of God, which makes it implicit that God is relational; it is his very nature to be in relationship, and it is his intention to have relationship with mankind whom he has created. This is emphasised by the fact that we have been made in the 'image' and 'likeness' of God. These words refer to *who* he is and *how* he is; they do not refer, as one might immediately think, to his appearance.

The Special Word

The second Bible theme is found in one of the last of the books in the New Testament, the first letter of John. Here we can read: "Whoever does not love does not know God, because God is love."[1] This is a striking statement – God is love – because it condenses everything that we can know about God into one attribute. Love is an inherently relational thing, especially this particular type of love. The New Testament part of the Bible was originally written in a popular form of the Greek language, known as 'koine' Greek. Unlike English, Greek uses three different words for love depending on the type of love being described. We are most familiar with two of these words, relating to 'tender affection' and 'romantic love'. In the present case however, the word used is a special form, 'agapé', which is hardly known from Greek literature other than the New Testament. Agapé has been described as the 'characteristic word of Christianity'. A dictionary of Bible words describes this type of love as "... an exercise of God's will in deliberate choice, made without obvious reason except that which lies in the nature of God himself."[2]

Potential for Frustration

If we hope to provide an answer to the present question that will satisfy us from the perspective of human motivations, then we will be frustrated because God is not like us in this – he is not driven in the ways that we are. If on the other hand we recognise that God is not tainted by our own human corruption, and that his motives are entirely pure, then we can see that his reaching out for relationship with us is entirely because it is his nature to do so.

The Lounge

Question 13 – Are men and women equal?

Being Different

The so-called 'battle of the sexes' isn't new, in fact it has been ongoing since mankind was first created. Why is there a battle? Essentially because there are differences. Do these differences make men and women unequal? Yes, of course they do. Men and women tend to have different strengths and different weaknesses, making them unequal in different respects. But these differences don't mean that men and women are of differing value, just that they are different, a difference that most people celebrate.

In reality these differences don't just occur between the sexes; they also occur within each gender. Some men are stereotypical 'he men' in physique or demeanour, while others are less physically robust or more sensitive or creative. Similarly, some women are stereotypically feminine, while others may be less so. Whatever the differences are, we may struggle to accommodate these and to fully value them – but that is our own problem. Do we need to face up to our prejudices?

Gender in the Bible

Within all of the books of the Bible, God is consistently referred to as male, whether the generic term 'God', or the individual persons of the Trinity (see the Study Room). Clearly Jesus is a man. But the use of the male personal pronoun doesn't mean that God is on the 'male side'. In fact, one of the attributes that the Bible associates with God is decidedly feminine – one of the names for God is the 'double breasted one' (Hebrew: El Shaddai).[1]

The position on gender that we see in the Bible is that man and woman are of equal value and are complementary. This is apparent in the story of the creation in the first book of the Bible, Genesis, and also in Jesus' ministry that we can read about in the four gospel accounts.[2] In fact, Jesus' dealings with women were revolutionary within the context of the culture of his day, a culture that did not always treat women as being of equal value to men.

Paul the Misogynist?

This brings us to the writings of the apostle Paul, the author of thirteen of the twenty-seven books of the New Testament. Some people think that Paul viewed women as inferior to men, but careful reading of Paul's letters shows us that this simply isn't true. In fact, he is perfectly clear that men and women are equal in God's sight.[3]

That being said, Paul does not shy away from addressing contentious topics about family relationships but faces them head-on, outlining God-given principles that form the basis for an effective working relationship between men and women.

If we were to consider certain specific comments of Paul, and take them in isolation, then they might not pass the test of modern-day political correctness. But this is an inappropriate way to handle any Bible passage; correct handling requires that every thought is taken in context within both the passage where it occurs, the overall teaching of the Bible, and to a lesser extent the cultural environment in which it is set. Yes, Paul says some things that many find hard to accept in relation to both women and men that can be challenging to both.[4] The bottom line is that Paul is not in the business of making things easy; his approach is to teach the truth, clearly and honestly, as God commissioned him to do.

Question 14 – Do all religions lead to God?

Selection Criteria

For someone who doesn't follow any faith this question is a pertinent one. Looking in from the outside, one might well view the variety of different world religions as a mere matter of choice – a case of evaluating each and choosing what we think to be the best, or which we feel is the better fit to our personal circumstances, world view or preferences. We might narrow down the options to create a shortlist, rather like interviewing for a job vacancy; perhaps we could reduce the 'religion' list to those that appear morally superior. But this approach presupposes that every religion leads to 'the God who is there', and that God doesn't mind which route we choose.

Alternatively, we might even be short-listing on the assumption that there isn't actually a God at all, and that religion is really about embracing an ethical system upon which to base our lives. Every answer in this book is predicated upon the understanding that the creator God does exist, that he is there and is also personally knowable by us. In answering the current question, we could be distracted into evaluating the moral superiority of the Christian faith. But this isn't the real issue.

Self-help Doesn't Cut It

Religions generally are based on the idea of self-improvement by one way or another; whether by gradually becoming more compliant to a code or to the demands of a deity, or by obedience to a set of rituals and practices. Christianity isn't like this. The Christian message is clear that we are not capable of winning any 'brownie points' with God – there is nothing that we can do to change ourselves and thereby win God's approval. Because of this the creator God has provided a way whereby the corrupted creation (us) can be reconciled to himself. We cannot do anything ourselves to repair the damage that our previous wrong decisions have caused, all we can do is to rely on God's provision for us, which is through the sacrifice that Jesus made when he died in our place.

A Radical Solution

The Christian story of how God made a way for us to have a relationship with himself is so radical that it precludes any alternatives; there is no scope for amalgamation with ideas from other religions, as some have tried to do. The claims of Christianity stand or fall on their own; they leave no room for an 'alternative' way to God. Just as it has been said that Jesus was either mad, bad or was actually God, so the Christian message, as contained in the New Testament part of the Bible, is either a deliberate deceit or it tells us about the one and only way to come into a living relationship with the Living God. This is highlighted by Jesus' assertion recorded in the Gospel according to John: "I am the way and the truth and the life. No one comes to the Father except through me."[1]

An Unacceptable Dichotomy

Some people have tried to disconnect the moral teaching of Jesus from the theology of Jesus, treating Jesus as merely a moral teacher and example of self-sacrifice. This approach is hugely subjective because it involves determining that one aspect of Jesus is good and the other bad – excellent moral philosophy but deceitful theology. This type of dichotomy is something that is exhibited in many religious systems but usually the other way around: embracing a theology in spite of the obvious moral shortcomings associated with the original messenger of the particular belief system. Christian faith allows no room for such hypocrisy; Jesus is everything that he claims to be. If this were not so then we would have to conclude that Jesus is a fake, the moral character of his message is compromised, and Christian faith is a sham.

It has to be acknowledged that Christianity has been tainted both by individuals and organisations that, while claiming to be Christian, have behaved as if they were not. However, the Christian message, which is clearly taught out from the pages of the New Testament, and the original messengers, are each above reproach in both substance and character.[2]

❖ Question 15 – How do Christians explain the existence of other religions?

Common Themes

One of the common themes within this book is the contrast between religion and genuine Christian faith. Just as there are many people who follow other religions, there are many who consider themselves to be Christian and yet become side-tracked into observing religious practices. Another of the common themes within this book is that there is only one God, and that there is only one way to have a relationship with him – through Jesus. If these assertions are actually true, then what should we make of other religions? Whilst religious people may be misguided, they are sincere and often passionate about their religion, and genuinely believe that they are living in the way that they should. The difficulty is that there is only one way to have a relationship with the Living God.

No Middle Ground

The writings in the New Testament part of the Bible make it very clear that God has provided a way for us to be reconciled to himself; he did this by sending his only son, Jesus, to pay the price of our wrongdoing when he was unjustly crucified. Jesus' death was a once-for-all-time sacrifice, made on behalf of us all, so that anyone who so chooses can ask God to forgive them and to set their lives on a new course through Jesus. We each have to decide what we believe, but if the Christian faith outlined in the words of the New Testament is not the only way to God, then it is deceitful – deceitful because this is exactly and unequivocally what it claims to be.[1] We have no choice other than to agree that Christian faith is the only way to God, or else to believe that it is a sham that cannot lead us to God at all. Christianity may be one of many 'religious systems', but it stands alone – it is untenable to suggest that Christianity is both true and also one of many ways to God. Given this, we need to see how 'other religions' fit within the Christian worldview.

People of Beauty

The Bible makes it clear that mankind was created by God in his own image; the obvious implication of this assertion is that we are very special beings who have certain God-like characteristics. Religion affords particular opportunity for expressing these characteristics, which is a reason why it has always been so compelling to people. In the Foundations question 'Who is God?' (Q 2), we considered how God gave mankind the ability not only to appreciate the beauty of what he has created, but also to create beautiful things ourselves. So often this ability has been used in the service of religion, and as a means of expressing religious ideas. This beauty, whether in the form of art, poetry, music or architecture, is enticing because it is an expression of God-given abilities. However, we must be clear that such expression, admirable as it may be in itself, reflects how God has made us – but it does not necessarily lead us to him. The fact that we create something that is undeniably beautiful doesn't mean that God is somehow 'in' it, or that he approves of what we intend the artistic expression to represent.[2]

Reaching Out

Obviously, Christians understand that the world holds many highly developed systems of religious belief but assert that it is only Christian faith, based on the New Testament, that can actually lead us to a relationship with God. Given this, we need to consider what these other religious systems actually are, and why they exist. The first conclusion is that they represent mankind's attempt to relate to God in some way. Some religions would assert that there are multiple deities rather than a single god, while others are not necessarily based on a belief of there being an actual deity. From a human perspective, religions are a way of reaching out to something beyond ourselves. This may be to a deity or deities who we hope will give meaning to our lives and help us, or it may be to some method whereby we feel we are living in harmony with the world around us.

Diversionary Tactics

There is another perspective that we need to consider, because it is crucial to appreciating the Christian understanding of other religions. Throughout the Bible, from the first few chapters to the last, we are clearly given to understand that there is more going on than we can see or appreciate. There are malevolent powers at work in the spiritual realm that are set against the Living God, that seek to thwart God's purpose for mankind, and are bent on steering people away from having the relationship with God that he intends for us (see the TV Room – Q 26 & 27). Given this, it is hardly surprising that multiple religions have sprung up since mankind's infancy. These 'alternative' religions attempt to feed mankind's thirst for spiritual fulfilment, but by doing so divert us from the truth, and also from coming into relationship with the Living God. From the perspective of the spiritual realm, 'alternative' religions are a diversionary tactic intended to distract us from what God has revealed in Jesus Christ. This applies to religious systems such as Islam and Hinduism for example, but also to pseudo-Christian belief systems such as Mormonism and Jehovah's Witnesses, amongst many others.

Is Judaism a Special Case?

The Christian faith is neither self-serving nor arrogant in claiming to be the only way to God. It is only asserting what Jesus himself is recorded as saying in the gospel accounts in the New Testament; that we can find forgiveness and peace with God through Jesus alone, and that God has neither provided nor sanctioned any other way.[3] This brings into focus something that we have kept clear of up till this point, but which needs addressing now: the question 'where does the Jewish faith fit in?'

A consideration of the Jewish faith is important for two reasons. Firstly, because Christianity arose from a background of Judaism; and secondly, because we need to consider what is the status of Judaism since the beginning of the Christian era.

The People of God

The Old Testament part of the Bible tells us that, from the beginning of human existence, God made ways for mankind to have a relationship with himself. This relationship was different to that which is enjoyed by Christians today, but it was a real relationship none the less. Over a very long period of time God made a series of relationship Covenants between himself and the people who honoured him. These people were genealogically linked and eventually became known as the Jewish nation. It was because of the failure of the Jewish people to serve God properly, and the inevitable estrangement from God that this brought about, that God promised to send a deliverer (the Messiah) for his people.[4] For the Jews there was a sting in the tail of this promise, because God made clear that when the deliverer came, deliverance would not only be available to the Jews but also to those who were not Jews (the Gentiles).[5] The Jews weren't happy about this because they were used to being the only 'People of God'. Jesus was the promised Messiah; he wasn't quite what many Jews had been hoping for, and the Jewish leaders refused to acknowledge who he truly was.

Christianity vs. Judaism

This sets the scene for where things stand today. From a Jewish perspective, Christianity is seen as something of a splinter movement based on what they regard as a 'heresy'. The Christian perspective is that Jesus is the Messiah of the Old Testament; he is the fulfilment of the great many promises that God made to his people the Jews. By this reckoning, Christian faith is the God-ordained continuation of the story of the people of God that we can read about in the Old Testament. It must be appreciated that the first Christians, large numbers of them, were Jewish believers who embraced the Messiah, Jesus. However, the religious authorities of the time did not – which is actually why they sponsored his judicial killing by their Roman rulers.

Is there Hope for the Jews?

So, how should we view adherents to the Jewish faith today? The charitable answer is to say that they are mistaken. However, one thing is for sure – that many have embraced the religious aspects of Jewish belief, but in rejecting the Messiah, Jesus, have disobeyed God. As there is no other mechanism whereby anyone can receive forgiveness from God, except through Jesus, we have to conclude that Jewish people are lost to God in the same way as followers of any other non-Christian religious system. Some Christians believe that the Jews will still, at some point, receive Jesus as their Messiah, and that through this they will come into a living relationship with God once again. All that we can say for certain is that, short of embracing Jesus the Messiah, Jewish faith does not provide any way to be reconciled to God. That said, it should be recognised that ever since the time of Jesus there have been Jews who have actually believed in their Messiah – starting with his disciples and the large numbers of Jewish Christians mentioned in the New Testament and continuing to this day. Becoming a Christian is a personal decision – for Jewish people as it is for every one of us, irrespective of whatever religious background we may come from.

Question 16 – What is the difference between religious observance and Christian faith?

Facing Facts

This is a difficult topic because there are multitudes of people who are very dedicated to following their religious practices and principles, and who sincerely believe that this is the right thing to do. It is hard to turn around and to discount such commitment and personal sacrifice, and yet we need to recognise that religious practices and active faith are not the same thing; the fact that someone is 'religious' doesn't necessarily mean that they have an active, living, faith in the Living God.[1]

Further, Christian faith can only exist on the basis of what God has revealed to us through the Bible. It has to be unconditional, not based on assumptions or upon a pick-and-mix selection of the truth. This point is particularly helpful in enabling us to understand how to differentiate between religious observance and authentic Christian faith. The history of the Christian church is littered with what we might think of as 'add-ons'; things that man has bundled in with the clear truth that God has revealed in the New Testament. The more obvious examples would be leadership hierarchies and religious dress, practices such as pilgrimages, the worship of 'saints' or the virgin Mary. There are many other subtler examples that would require a whole new book to outline! These 'add-ons' have an unfortunate impact, resulting in a church landscape that may appear confused, one that sometimes presents an incoherent message.

What Went Wrong?

A long time ago my wife Jean and I found ourselves in a position where we felt that we had little choice but to leave the church that we were members of, and in which we had held leadership roles. This was a very difficult time; we felt let down, unfairly judged, and uncared for. During the weeks that followed our departure, I gave a lot of thought to what had occurred, and what might be the reasons behind this – both within us and within this particular church. Part of my review involved considering what it was about this church that seemed to be 'of God', and what it was that seemed to be due to tradition or 'religiousness'. Please don't get me wrong, this was essentially a good church, but there was still a degree of compromise with religion about it.

The Problem of Compromise

This compromise is nothing new, we see similar things occurring throughout the Bible, whether in the Old Testament or the New – people going 'off message' and adding their own ideas to what God has said.[2] One of the areas of compromise that was a real problem for the church right from the start of Christianity was that some converts from the Jewish religion wanted the new Christians to comply with certain Jewish rituals. They were effectively seeking to synchronise Christian faith with Old Testament Jewish practice. In his New Testament letters, the apostle Paul can be seen arguing against this attempt to carry over incompatible ideas and practices from the Old Testament religion. Paul recognised the danger; he saw that such compromise would fatally undermine the Christian message of freedom and liberation through Jesus.[3] This would mean people relying once again on the same sort of 'rules' as characterised Old Testament religion, and by doing this their acceptability to God would become based on whether or not they could comply with these rules (which the Jewish people had never fully been able to). The Christian message is that our acceptability to God is based on our asking for his forgiveness for our wrongdoing; this forgiveness is available through Jesus alone, based solely on the sacrifice that he made when he died in our place on the cross. Jewish rules and Christian faith are incompatible.

A Simple Formula

So, what is the difference between 'religion' and 'faith'? No doubt some people will choose to define this differently, but for me there is a clear formula – faith is what we do in direct obedience to what God has actually asked of us; religion is anything that we add to this or use as a substitute for it. Following this definition, it is clear that faith is a good thing. Obedience to God can only be good. Equally, we need to be very cautious about any attempt to change what God has said, whether by re-interpreting or by adding things that are not fully compatible with New Testament truth.

An Evolved Praxis

Many religious people add to what is revealed in the Bible, citing church tradition as a basis for Christian practice, but this is where compromise so readily gets in. For instance, some Christian traditions rely on a 'priesthood' to act like a middle man between us and God. There was a sense of this in the religious practices outlined in the Old Testament, but this idea is entirely at odds with the message and teaching of the New Testament – the Christian message. Here God calls people into a personal, individual, relationship with himself, not through a religious 'priesthood' that act as intermediaries, but solely through the one intermediary whom God himself appointed, Jesus Christ.[4]

Taming God

As discussed within the Foundations section, under the topic 'What is a Christian?' (Q 1), we are inherently religious beings, and yet we are also spoiled beings. Putting these characteristics together we find that mankind tends to want to tame God; to limit his call upon our lives such that it is us who remain in full control, albeit following rituals that are intended as a means of placating God. Religious people keep God in the box that they call 'my religion' or 'my church', elevating the box, but not elevating God himself; they will practice religion but without allowing God free access to their lives.

The message of the Bible, from beginning to end, is that God wants to be in relationship with us, and that this entails our hearts and wills being in tune with him. We are called to trust God completely, to follow his leading at whatever cost to ourselves. This is when we know that we are exercising faith, and not merely being religious.

Question 17 – Will people who believe in other faiths still go to heaven?

Playing by the Rules

Every game has rules that the players have to comply with. When a player steps onto the pitch, or court, he understands that the game he engages in is bound by rules. The player may not like them, or may not even understand why some of them are there, but knows that he has to follow them to compete in the game. A runner competing on the athletics track knows that if she leaves the blocks before the starter's pistol is fired, then she is likely to be disqualified. The long jumper knows that if he oversteps the launch mark then his jump will be invalid.

When it comes to religious belief, the situation isn't so very different to a sport or athletics event; each religion has some understanding of how adherents are expected to conduct themselves so as to be considered to have 'played by the rules'. The difficulty is that whilst religious systems can formulate whatever rules they choose to recognise, this doesn't oblige God to accept those same rules. This just goes to show that we live in a mixed-up world where, instead of finding out what God requires, we expect that he will accept what we humans decide to set in place.

The Long Wait

In the Bible, in the Old Testament book of Exodus, there is a story that highlights the need to 'play by God's rules'. This story tells of what happened when Moses, whom God had chosen to lead his people out of Egypt and into the land that he had promised to them, met with God on Mount Sinai. It seems that Moses was on the mountain with God for rather a long time, and the vast number of people who had escaped from Egypt with him were at the foot of the mountain waiting for him to come back down to them with words from God. They lost patience and, choosing to assume that Moses had died on the mountain, demanded that Aaron the priest make them other 'gods' who they could worship. Astonishingly Aaron complied with their request, making a large golden idol in the form of a calf.

When Moses eventually came back down the mountain, he discovered the golden calf and realised that the people had so readily turned away from worshipping God. This was the Living God who had brought them out of Egypt by means of a series of astonishing miracles (the plagues of Egypt), had caused the Red Sea to part enabling them to cross on dry land, and had been leading them up to this point.[1] Without going into detail, it is sufficient to note that there were serious consequences for the people who had turned from worshipping the Living God to worshipping a golden idol made by man.

Let's Get Serious

The moral of this Bible story is that God is not to be trifled with. We get to choose what we believe, and how we respond to God, but there are consequences for 'doing our own thing', including if we choose to follow 'alternate' faiths. So to answer the question about our future destiny, we have to understand that the way to heaven is through having a relationship now with the God who is there, a relationship that is freely available to us through Jesus alone.[2] A friend of mine made a highly pertinent comment when he asked the rhetorical question: "Why would anyone want to spend eternity with God in heaven, but not want to have a relationship with him now?" My friend is surely correct – this makes no sense at all.

Question 18 – If God is loving, why doesn't he 'save' everyone?

Falling at the First Hurdle

In the first pages or the Bible, in the book of Genesis, there is an account of the creation of everything, including the creation of the first man and the first woman, Adam and Eve. This account moves straight on to introduce a fundamental theme that runs through all of the pages of the Bible, namely, the theme of human freedom to choose and the implications of bad choices. This is far more than a mere morality tale; the message of those early chapters of Genesis is that mankind has been permanently tainted and spoiled by a single choice that Adam and his wife made. The story of Genesis is that our ancestors chose to defy God, to deliberately and knowingly disobey the one simple rule that he had given to them to follow.[1]

Consequences

We are told that the immediate effect of this action for Adam and Eve was that they felt shame for the first time, became conscious of their nakedness and joined fig leaves together to form rudimentary garments to cover their bodies.[2] This was the effect that their action had within themselves, but there were other, major consequences that were imposed on them by God.[3] The question we have to ask is 'why God would do that?' The answer is because it was something that these first people needed if their behaviour was to be moderated in future. Otherwise both they and their descendants would become people who were totally without constraint, lawless and godless. We read that God took the steps that he did because they were necessary for the benefit of mankind – he took them because of his love for the people whom he had created.

The linking of love and discipline is a clear Bible theme that is stated explicitly in both the Old Testament and the New Testament.[4] We often get confused and think that discipline is an act of unkindness, whereas in reality it is the exact opposite that is true. Where discipline is called for, then to withhold it is an act of selfishness and, not to put too strong a point on it, actually an expression of hatred. We find this taught in the wisdom literature within the Bible, in the book of Proverbs: "If you refuse to discipline your son, it proves you don't love him; for if you love him, you will be prompt to punish him."[5]

Getting to Choose

Freedom of choice is fundamental to God's purpose for us. He doesn't force us to honour or worship him, either by compelling us or by stacking the odds in his own favour. If we are to become worshippers of God then it is to be a deliberate choice on our part – we have this choice to make, and responsibility for the outcome of our choice is also ours. Under the previous topic we concluded that we can't expect to make our own rules about what is acceptable to God. By the same reasoning we can't expect God to set aside the consequences that he has decreed for our wrong choices. Yes, of course we are weak and flawed; obviously we make mistakes and may fail to realise the consequences of our actions. God knows this only too well, which is why he provided a flawless way whereby our relationship with him is able to be restored – a restoration that is freely available to us through his son, Jesus. This is God's offer to every one of us; not that he will choose to ignore our failures, but that he will deal with the consequences for us – if we ask him to.[6]

Tainted

The bottom line is that we are tainted people – every one of us; the Bible makes it plain that nobody is perfect.[7] But then we know this for ourselves don't we? It isn't startling news. Some people may appear to behave well if compared to most others, but every one of us is flawed and unfit to be in God's presence. This is why God cannot simply brush aside our wrongdoing and accept everyone. There is a way to be reconciled to God, but it is God's way, and there is only one way. Each of us has to decide – we have the freedom to choose – whether or not to accept, on God's terms, the offer he makes to us. So, the reason that God doesn't 'save' everyone is because not everyone wants to be saved. Restoration of our relationship with God is available to anyone, through what Jesus did for us when he surrendered to an unjust death on a Roman cross some 2000 years ago.

Question 19 – Is atheism a religious belief?

Not so Simple

If you are someone whose understanding of atheism is that it is simply the belief that God does not exist, then this question may appear rather odd, or at least you may anticipate a very clear and straightforward answer. In reality, atheism can have more in common with religious belief than you might think.

Believe What You Will

There have always been people who, for one reason or another, have concluded that belief in God is a delusion that they are careful to steer clear of. But we should distinguish between such a traditional atheistic perspective and the more dogmatic form of atheism that has been peddled in recent times by the likes of Richard Dawkins, which has been referred to as the 'New Atheism'. Some people, who are not atheists, will declare themselves to be agnostic, being uncertain of what to believe about the existence of God – an entirely honest position as far as it goes. Some will declare themselves atheist, believing that God does not exist – another honest position. However, some who believe that there is no God are dogmatic in their assertion; they preach their message and argue vociferously for their entrenched position – not so honest this one, because it is a 'faith' position, based on an un-provable assertion.

Atheistic or Anti-Religious?

This strident form of atheistic belief does actually manifest itself like a religion. In a similar way to how Christians want to share with other people the truth that they have come to know about God, and to share their personal experience of relationship with God, so dogmatic atheists proclaim a message that denies God and strives for a freedom from religious constraints. Maybe this last point is the crux of the matter – religious constraints. Often the most ardent detractors are those who have a religious background; they may have been hurt or damaged by religious dogma, judgemental attitudes or religious falsehood, or simply been hurt through the circumstances of life and cannot accept that God would allow these things to occur.

Crusaders

Whatever the motivation, there are people today who are unwilling to simply state their position as 'unbelievers' but are insistent that they are right and are on a mission to swing everyone else to their position. They seek self-justification by stridently opposing Christianity as a matter of atheistic dogma. They ardently pursue their religious crusade, attempting to disprove that which they themselves are unwilling to accept. With clear similarity to Bible-believing Christians who seek to tell other people about their faith – a faith in something (or rather someone) – the New Atheists proclaim their non-belief in God as though this was the logical position to adopt. Their ardour seems strange; at least it does until we recognise that the position they are promoting is actually a faith-based position, and if that is true then it is also a religious belief, albeit based on something other than God.

Question 20 – What if the media puts me off God?

A Difficult Job

To be fair we must acknowledge that the role of public broadcasters is not an easy one when it comes to 'religious' broadcasting. They are supposed to be non-partisan; they strive to meet a broad spectrum of taste and of religious tradition, and at the end of the day are driven by viewing/ listening numbers. In England there is the 'Established' church, the Church of England, and perhaps it is to be expected that programmes will in the main be orientated towards this. That said, with few brilliant exceptions, what is broadcast is at best mediocre, and not likely to encourage anyone to take Christian faith seriously. While there may be no easy answers for the broadcasters, it is hard not to be in sympathy with those who respond to the broadcast material by saying that "if this is Christianity then I don't want anything to do with it". However, it is important to emphasis at this point that genuine, wholehearted Christian belief, which is firmly based on the truth of what the Bible tells us, is quite different to the typical media depiction.

Cultural Expectations

So far we have only considered programmes that come under the 'religious' remit, but of course this isn't the only place where faith is depicted in the broadcast media. For many people Christian faith is an important part of their lives, and popular programming tends to reflect this, albeit often in a distorted way. So we may come across characters in drama programmes that are intended to reflect a form of Christianity: bland vicars, eccentrics or bigots. Then there are the docudramas that are based on the activity within a church parish somewhere or other. Pleasant, and perhaps interesting as well, their focus tends to be 'religiousness' – but then maybe that is all that can realistically be expected: a lowest common denominator depiction.

Genre Broadcasting

Lastly, we need to recognise that many homes now have access to a wide range of programming: traditional broadcast channels, advertising/selling based channels, etc., and also dedicated religious channels. The latter show some excellent and highly reputable programmes; but sadly, because of their general nature, some air content that reflects badly upon Christian faith. This may be because of distorted views that reflect an unbalanced understanding of the Bible, or because they adopt emotionally charged tactics in the hope of getting a response from viewers, or due to their making inappropriate calls for financial donations.

Let's Get Radical

From any of these things it is reasonable to be offended and you might well feel disinclined to look further at Christian faith. However, it is important to note that these often limp, and sometimes despicable, depictions have little bearing on what God is truly like, what the church is supposed to be like, or what individual Christians are called by God to be like. Christian faith is not about 'religiousness' but a real and dynamic relationship with the Living God; it is not a crutch to help people through life, but power to fulfil God's purpose and his commission in the lives of individual Christians. What is depicted in the broadcast media is sometimes weak, distorted, lifeless and unattractive. Real Christianity is powerful, radical and revolutionary.[1] Someone might well be offended by this, but at least that would be a reaction to God, rather than to how Christian faith has been falsely caricatured.

Question 21 – How can Christians be so confident in their faith?

Facing Reality

To exercise faith is to make a commitment based on understanding and experience. During the Second World War many Londoners took refuge in the underground railway system whenever they heard the wail of the air raid sirens. This wasn't a comfortable choice to make, but the people knew that the stations deep below the city streets were safe places to be, no matter what horrendous damage the bombing raid was inflicting up above on the surface. The people knew from experience that when the sirens sounded, there was a raid coming, and they fled to safety – they exercised faith. When the siren made a different noise, sounding the 'all clear', the people knew that it was now safe to leave the security of the underground network and return to their homes, places of work, schools, etc. In doing so they may well have witnessed something of the damage that the bombs had inflicted, reaffirming to them the rightness of their earlier decision to seek shelter in response to the siren's wail.

A Sound Foundation

The exercise of Christian faith is not unlike the faith of those Londoners; it is a commitment based on understanding and experience. Our friend Clare became a Christian after completing her degree course. Her experience while at university had been peculiar; she was doggedly atheistic, but found herself in the company of Christians at every turn – Christians who told her about God's love, tried to encourage her to consider the claims of Christianity, and prayed unceasingly that she too would become a Christian. Clare was determined that this wasn't for her, and resisted vigorously, even starting up a 'Heathen Union' in an attempt to counteract the university Christian Union.

It wasn't until after her time at university that Clare came to be so in awe of how intricately and beautifully formed the human body is, that she realised that the only sustainable explanation for this was God. Clare was confronted by the work of God's hand; she recognised him in his creation.

Before making a decision to commit our lives to God, we need to have a sound basis for exercising faith; it is a big commitment that requires a solid foundation. Clare knew the facts of Christianity from her university days, but for these to become real for her she needed to be convinced.

Clare's story is not unlike that of the apostle Paul who we read about in the New Testament. Paul was stridently anti-Christian and was determined to snuff out this new, fledgling faith; he colluded with the Jewish religious authorities who licensed him to persecute and imprison Christians. Paul's change of heart was brought about by a dramatic encounter when travelling to the city of Damascus to continue his persecution there – his 'Damascus Road' experience. During this encounter he heard Jesus speaking to him directly, and he realised that Jesus was indeed the son of God, and the Christian message was actually true.[1]

More Than Conviction

Like the Londoners acting to take shelter during the war, people become Christians when they act upon their convictions, take God at his word and accept the forgiveness that he offers and the new life that he promises to those who will follow and obey him. They may be convinced by any number of things: the wonders of God's creation, the truth of the Bible message, or some direct experience of God – or a combination of these. But this isn't the whole picture. Once acted upon, understanding becomes supported by experience. For the Londoners it was the experience of being kept safe, and indeed feeling safe, and the experience of what they had been saved from once they returned to the surface and saw the destruction. For the Christian there are different types of experience that reinforce their initial faith.

Forgiveness

The message of Christianity is that God will forgive us for everything that we have ever done wrong – if we ask him, based on what Jesus did for us when he gave up his life by dying for us on the cross. Many people, who take this step of coming to God and seeking forgiveness, actually experience the weight of their sin, guilt and shame, being lifted and removed. They know that God has forgiven them, that what was promised has really happened.

76

This is both an initial experience and an ongoing one. When we take the step of becoming a Christian it is only the start of a journey; we are still flawed human beings, will still do things that are not pleasing to God, and will need to ask to be forgiven regularly.

Direction and Guidance

God wants people to come into a relationship with him by believing, exercising faith and receiving forgiveness, but that is only a part of it. God also calls us to commit our lives to honouring him, and as part of this, to serving him. Given such a commitment, we then need to know what he wants us to do; this is where direction and guidance comes in. Christians experience God's ongoing direction in their lives. This may come about in many different ways, all of which amount to the same thing – being convinced that God has shown them something that they need to act upon. Like the Londoners surfacing after an air raid who could see tangible evidence for the rightness of their decision to seek shelter, Christians look back on key moments in their lives when they knew that God was directing them – spiritual milestones.

Intervention

An amazing privilege that Christians have is the ability to ask God to act, the freedom to approach him through prayer and to make requests. This isn't just some sort of spiritual exercise; it is real and evidenced by these prayers being answered and his response seen.

So when we ask how Christians can be so confident in their faith, the answer comes down to understanding, conviction and experience. Understanding the truth, being convinced of it, and experiencing the outcome when faith is exercised. Christians can look back to the day when they first experienced God's forgiveness and came into a relationship with him. They can look back to other milestones in their journey with God when he has clearly directed them or has intervened in their lives in some very obvious way. Christians can look back to times when they have called out to God in prayer and they have seen his intervention in the circumstance that they brought to him. They can look back to knowing God walking with them through the difficulties and challenges of life.

When Christians experience the reality of God in their lives, they have every reason to have confidence in his ongoing faithfulness as they face the future. This not only applies to the days and years ahead, but also to what the Bible has to tell us about death and the life beyond the grave as well.

Question 22 – Why do some Christians use strange words and expressions?

Strange Language

All specialist areas tend to have their own specific terminology, and Christian faith is no exception. For instance, there are concepts that have technical names, such as 'salvation', and there is a naming and indexing convention for referencing Bible passages. There are also many names of people and places mentioned in the Bible with which Christians become familiar over time. These types of specialist knowledge are difficult to avoid; they go with the territory. There are, however, other terms and expressions that are not necessary.

Unnecessary Barriers

From the very start it has been part of the mission of the church to reach out to other people with the message of Jesus: the message of forgiveness and reconciliation to God. The apostle Paul in his extensive missionary enterprise worked hard to overcome religiousness and to call the church to remain focussed on the spiritual essentials. In Paul's context it wasn't language that was the issue but religious traditions and practices. However, the same principle pertains. Why create unnecessary and unhelpful barriers for people? The mission of Christians today is focussed on communicating the message of God's love and purpose, just as it was for Paul. This message in itself is obstacle enough for people without adding other unhelpful and unnecessary hurdles.[1] I want to suggest three reasons why some people use strange language: holiness, history and habit.

Holiness

There is the idea that things related to God are 'holy'; that is, set apart, different to the everyday. This is not unreasonable. God is certainly holy, and anything related to God should be handled with respect. However, we need to return to the differentiation between what is truly spiritual and what is merely religious. There is a danger that what is religious is treated as holy or special. But by doing this, important spiritual imperatives are undermined. Strange language is a case in point. The problem of 'strange words and expressions' is largely due to mankind's religious nature; our inclination is to take something that is pure and powerful, and to tame it, ritualising it in the process. You might consider this reasonable, but it actually hinders communication, and can therefore undermine the spiritual mission of the church to spread the message of Jesus to those who don't yet know him.

History

The study of geology entails understanding how various types of structure were formed over long periods of time; mineral deposits being laid down, layer upon layer, resulting in the landscape features that we can see and experience. There has been a tendency for the Christian church to do something similar, allowing the layers to build up over time to create something that appears to have substance in itself. The resulting religious landscape includes complicated concepts and language that may set the church apart, but also separates it from the 'normal' and makes it strange and difficult to access to those for whom it is unfamiliar. In other contexts, we see the processes that formed our geology as negative. For instance, we seek to avoid or remove any build-up of lime scale from shower heads; we prefer to see the shiny chromium as it was originally formed, and to have the water spray undiminished. Anything that is an impediment to the clear and effective communication of God's message must be suspect; surely strange language is to be avoided.

Habit

We can recognise that for those who have grown up within a 'church' environment, all of the 'strange' language is very familiar; they are comfortable with it and to them it is entirely normal. In fact, it can be just as hard for them to separate themselves from this way of speaking as it is for other people to understand this language. But this doesn't change the fact that Christians are commissioned to spread the 'good news' about Jesus, and the use of specialist, or just old-fashioned, language is an impediment to this.

Example

The New Testament was originally written in Greek, not formal, classical Greek but a variant of the language that was spoken commonly across the whole of the Roman Empire. This was the everyday language of the ordinary people. Because of this the New Testament writings were accessible to everyone who could read, or who heard the words being read; the language was down to earth and readily understood. Anyone who uses strange language today, thinking that it is somehow more appropriate for conversations about God, is actually out of step with the writers of the New Testament.

Question 23 – If I became a Christian would I have to become 'religious'?

Being Religious

The immediate answer to this is "definitely not, please don't!" But then we should consider exactly what we mean by 'religious'.

Throughout this book, the term 'religious' is used as a negative term; religion being defined as something that man does apart from actually having a relationship with God. Accordingly, being 'religious' is used to mean doing things that at best are not essential to such a relationship, and at worst have the effect of obscuring what God wants for us, substituting the artificial for the genuine.

The 'Inner Me'

Rather than thinking about the negative aspects of being religious, it is more helpful for us to consider what positive responses God wants to encourage from someone once they have become a Christian and have committed their lives to him.

Some people make the mistake of thinking that it is external behaviour that needs to change in us; but actually, God is concerned about the 'inner me'. Where our inner selves are set free and get into line with what God has to tell us, then our outward behaviour will inevitably change in response. Religious people tend to emphasise the externals, requiring others to comply with a sometimes arbitrary code of conduct; God is concerned about what is going on in our hearts.[1] Religious people tend to separate themselves from the world around; God wants Christians to be his ambassadors in the world[2] – to be there amongst everyone else, but governed by his principles rather than being driven by those of the world around them. In the New Testament the apostle Paul writes about the need for Christians to allow God to 'renew their minds'.[3] That is, to set things straight, according to what is true and wholesome, and what reflects the work of God in their hearts.

What Changes?

There are things that often do change in people after they become Christians – good changes that are brought about by a transformation in the person's heart attitude – such as no longer using blasphemous or coarse language. Someone who has been prone to dishonesty may become truthful. Someone who was previously inclined to take things that were not theirs may stop doing this; they might even feel that they should return such items to their rightful owner. All of these changes can come about as a result of someone becoming a Christian and having a change of heart. Does this amount to becoming religious? – of course it doesn't.

Natural Responses

There are other changes in behaviour that people who become Christians tend to exhibit. Usually the start of a relationship with God means that the person wants to get to know God better; just like a newly married couple will take opportunities to spend time together. It would be rather strange if they didn't want to do this. In the case of a Christian this may include wanting to know what the Bible says, wanting to talk with God in prayer and wanting to be with other Christians. For some this may sound 'religious', but it is the natural outworking of the new relationship. These desires are a heart response to God.

There is one other thing that new Christians often want to do; they want to tell other people about what they themselves have discovered – that God is real – and about what this has meant to their lives. If you discover something that was hidden from you before, something that you come to realise is of great importance, then it is only natural to want to share this experience or knowledge with family, friends and work colleagues. The Christian who does this may well be accused of being 'religious', but actually they will only be telling the truth about what they have experienced; there is nothing strange about doing that – it is a natural response, an overflowing of the heart.

Question 24 – Why can't Christians keep quiet about Jesus?

Four Good Men

There is a Bible story in the Old Testament that I am particularly fond of, which is told in the second book of Kings.[1] This passage records that the city of Samaria had been besieged by the Aramean army for a considerable time, and things were desperate for the inhabitants. At this point God's prophet Elijah tells the people that by the same time the following day, food will be sold cheaply in the city – something that appeared to be totally impossible. The story goes that there were four men who were suffering from leprosy, who were staying just outside of the gate of the city (presumably because they were outcasts due to their affliction). These men reasoned that as things stood, they were destined to die; whether they stayed put or even if they went into the city they would die from hunger.

So, they decided to take their lives into their own hands and surrender to the Arameans, reasoning that it was possible that they would be spared, but if not, then their fate would be no worse than if they stayed where they were. Late that day they went over to the camp of the Arameans, only to find that nobody was there – God had caused their enemy to flee in panic, leaving the camp just as it was without taking anything with them. Understandably, these lepers took the opportunity to eat and drink all that they wanted; they also found some valuables in the enemy tents and hid them. But then they realised that they were wrong to benefit from this great deliverance and not let the people in the beleaguered city know what God had done for them, thereby enabling all of the inhabitants of Samaria to benefit as they themselves had done.

Illustration

This story is from the Old Testament, and relates to a practical circumstance, but it mirrors very well the situation in which Christians find themselves. This story tells us in vivid terms why Christians can't keep quiet about Jesus.

The Bible makes clear to us that we will all face the judgement of God when we die. We will all face the penalty for the wrong that we have done. The difference for someone who is a Christian, someone who has been forgiven by God, is that Jesus has taken the penalty upon himself – they have no debt to pay. The lepers from Samaria are like those who ask God for mercy and are thereby freed from their circumstances. When someone becomes a Christian and discovers that the freedom they are offered through Jesus is for real, they want to tell others who have yet to experience this. They want to encourage other people to find out for themselves the great deliverance that God has provided through the sacrifice of his son, Jesus.

Motivations

Some Christians are particularly motivated because they realise that people they care about – family, friends or colleagues – are destined for an eternal existence separated from God. Others simply recognise God's love for mankind, and Jesus' sacrifice, and think that this is news that everyone should have the chance to know about and respond to.

If you had discovered something that was immensely beneficial to your life, and realised that others could gain a similar benefit, wouldn't you want to let them know? There is however another very important reason why Christians want to tell other people the good news about Jesus. This is because Jesus left his followers with instructions to do just that; in telling others about Jesus they are quite simple being obedient to him.[2]

The Television Room

 Question 25 – What is heaven like?

Welsh Harps

The images of heaven that are sometimes portrayed can be misleading, such as the idea that those who 'go to heaven' will spend their time sitting on fluffy clouds and playing Welsh harps. Sometimes heaven is imagined to be a paradise, like a carefree existence on a remote, sun-drenched Pacific island.

It is difficult to understand what heaven is actually like. We can be influenced by whatever preconceived ideas we may have, but we also need to recognise that our one reliable source of information about heaven, the Bible, gives only a partial glimpse – we are not given a full picture. Some people try to extrapolate from particular things that the Bible does tell us, but this can result in various exaggerated and distorted ideas that are inconsistent with the Bible generally and are consequently unreliable. In order to form a basis for understanding what heaven is like, we need to start by considering what we can reliably glean from the Bible.

Where to Go

We are given to understand that heaven is the dwelling place of God, and that his presence pervades heaven. This understanding is fundamental. We refer to people 'going to heaven' when their life on earth comes to its conclusion. For those who have chosen to love and serve God during their lifetimes it makes sense that they should then go to the place where God is. It makes equal sense that those who have not loved God and have chosen to live for their own pleasure instead of pleasing God, will go somewhere else – not the place where God's presence is.

New Responsibility

The Bible separates the idea of responsibility and work from the difficulties and toil that work entails. We tend to think that heaven will not be a place of toil, but in thinking this we can get the idea that there won't be responsibility or work either. This is an incorrect understanding. We read at the beginning of the first book in the Bible, the book of Genesis, that when God made man, he placed him in the Garden of Eden and gave him both work and responsibility:

> The Lord God took the man and put him in the Garden of Eden to work it and take care of it.[1]

The words 'to work' in this verse are variously shown by different Bible translators as: 'to cultivate', 'to tend', 'to farm'. The bottom line is that, even in the paradise of the Garden of Eden, there was work to be done. The important thing to note is that this wasn't arduous toil. Toil was something that came about as a result of mankind's succumbing to temptation and defying God; toil was something that God introduced after our ancestor's time in Eden, as a means of constraining mankind.[2]

When we consider what this 'work' in heaven might consist of, we find that the Bible specifically refers to 'judging' and 'reigning'.[3] Given that we have little idea of what heaven itself is actually like, it is difficult to appreciate quite what is intended here, except that there will be things to do and responsibilities to fulfil. What we can certainly glean from the Bible is that there are huge numbers of spiritual beings of various types who inhabit heaven, so the idea of God's people 'reigning' isn't so strange.

All Things New

Let's now consider what heaven itself might be like. Some religious people make a big thing about heaven, about life after death and what will happen to the 'creation' at the end of time. They attempt to be precise about the unclear, which is rather sad. Firstly, it is sad because we have no reason to be concerned about the future; God wants us to love him and serve him now – if we trust him now then we can trust him with our future as well. And secondly, because the Bible is so unclear; surely if it was important for us to have a detailed understanding about the future, then God would have ensured that the Bible was much clearer on this. If it was important for us to know, then the Bible would give us a precise and consistent picture of just what the future will be like.

What is both definite and clear from the Bible is that the world will come to an end one day; it will be destroyed, and we cannot know when this will be.[4] Also, we can understand that our existence in heaven will be at least as 'real' as our existence now. When we think of heaven, we can easily imagine somewhere ethereal and unsubstantial – but this isn't the understanding that we get from what the Bible does tell us. The heaven of the Bible is a place of substance, a different substance to what we are accustomed to, but just as real. The Bible speaks of a 'new heaven' and a 'new earth', and also of us having new, spiritual bodies. In fact, we should expect to be aware of a greater sense of reality in heaven than in our current existence. We will be in God's presence. We won't be burdened with the frailties of our fleshly existence – the complexities of mental and emotional stresses, tears and physical pain. And we won't be in competition with one another.

Bottom Line

Obviously, this is referring to heaven – not the 'other place'. Our destination is ultimately in God's hands, it is his decision. However, the message of the Bible is that those who choose to love and serve God in this life will be accepted into heaven because of their reliance on what Jesus did for them when he died in their place. On the other hand, those who reject Jesus on earth are, by doing so, determining their own eternal destiny somewhere other than heaven.[5]

❖ Question 26 – Is there a Devil?

Comic Image

Popular mythology has an image of a devil with horns, a tail and carrying a trident; an image used in comedy and horror movies, but not to be taken for real. That devil does not exist. But is there any substance behind the idea of a malevolent spiritual being, and if so, what is the truth?

The only way to answer this question is from a Christian perspective, because it is within the Bible that we find a clear description of who the devil is and of what he is like. We don't need to exercise our imaginations to conjure up an explanation, it is plain to see. The message of the Bible is that the devil certainly does exist, but that he is nothing like the image we see in popular media, nor for that matter like the carved stone gargoyles of medieval cathedrals. We need to clear these thoughts from our minds and start from basics.

We are Not Alone

Astronomers are going to great lengths in their search for life on other planets, seeking to discover whether or not we are truly alone in the cosmos. The Bible tells us that we are most certainly not alone – not that there is life that is anything like ours 'out there', but that there are other, spiritual beings. Indeed, these spiritual beings are not so very far from us. This understanding is summed up by the apostle Paul in one of his New Testament letters:

> For our struggle is not against flesh and blood, but against the rulers, against the authorities, against the powers of this dark world and against the spiritual forces of evil in the heavenly realms.[1]

Here Paul writes about malevolent spiritual forces, at work in our world and also in the heavenly realm. Most of the time we are unaware of these forces, but Paul assures us that they do in fact exist, and are opposed to us in some way; hence his mention of a struggle. We can see from what the Bible tells us that Satan (the devil) does not stand alone; he leads a multitude of spirit followers who are like him, and who do his bidding.

What's His Game?

There are different words used in the Bible to refer to the devil. The term 'devil' is probably the one that most people are familiar with; other terms used are 'Satan' and 'Beelzebub'. They obviously have different meanings but are still referring to the same spiritual being. The term devil means the 'accuser' or 'slanderer'. The term Satan means the 'adversary'. The term Beelzebub means 'prince of demons'. Christians are probably more inclined to use the term Satan because of its meaning and because it is the more frequently used term in the Bible.

The Bible tells us that Satan was one of the chief angels in heaven, but that he rebelled against God, and was followed in this by many lower level angelic beings. These form a force that is opposed to God and that resists God's will, both in the heavenly realm and on the earth. This is a rather different picture to the comical devil that we are familiar with, however this one is the reality. Satan has one single focus – to oppose God, and as part of this to oppose those who obey God and to hold captive those who do not obey God.[2]

Expectations

We have considered under other topics how God is very different to us, and that we cannot expect him to fit in with our understanding, perspectives or ideas of what he 'should' be like. There is a sense in which the same principle applies to the devil, or Satan – he probably doesn't fit our expectations. Satan is not a mischievous fiend or a lovable rogue. He has one purpose and that is to stand in opposition to God. As part of his opposition to God he does everything he can to thwart God's plan for mankind. He is the master of duplicity, the arch deceiver, the archetypal malevolent schemer.[3]

Total Warfare

During the Second World War, the British Prime Minister, Winston Churchill, realised that to have any chance of successfully standing against the power of the German Third Reich the British had to be totally committed to the fight. Hard decisions had to be made based on a single-minded focus upon the required end result. There wasn't any room for military niceties – this was a kill-or-be-killed situation involving the whole British nation, and ultimately the future of Europe too. In the midst of this, Churchill ordered the Royal Navy to do something almost unthinkable – to sink the French Mediterranean fleet that was sitting in port in Algeria so as to prevent it falling into German hands. This was total warfare.

Who Wrote the Book?

Total warfare is what Satan is involved in – but in this instance it is he who is the 'bad guy' and, along with his followers, is committed to total warfare against God himself. In opposing God he has burned his bridges; there is no turning back for him, and there is no 'playing nice'. He may be behind some things that we often think of as generally good, such as some religion, and he may not be behind many things that we tend to consider as evil, such as some warfare. Satan is not playing a game – he and his demonic hordes are deadly serious. They have set themselves against God and, in their attempt, are ready to employ every trick in the book – in fact they probably wrote the book. One such trick is the comic 'devil' that we started out with – a caricature, an image to deflect us from understanding who and what the devil truly is. He is opposed to God, opposed to the Christian church, and opposed to you – whether you are a Christian or not. There is nothing at all good about Satan. But there is some good news concerning him – he will not win.[4] The Bible tells us that Satan and his followers were defeated through Jesus' death and resurrection. He is still there, still a very real force to be reckoned with, but his days are numbered; God has already handed down the sentence.[5]

Question 27 – Does evil exist and, if so, what is it?

What Do We Mean?

'Evil' is a term that we may find ourselves using without thinking much about precisely what we are saying. The term can have different meanings depending upon the context in which it is used, and also upon the outlook of the person using it. Whilst we all understand that the word 'evil' is used to describe something that is bad, there are different types of 'bad'. We may, for instance, consider that hard work is a 'necessary evil'. We may also think that terrorists are evil, or at least do evil acts. Hopefully we all recognise the Holocaust as an extreme example of an act that is evil through and through. And we may also appreciate that there is evil in the spiritual realm. Science fiction fans may recall the idea in Star Wars, where the 'Empire' is depicted as malevolent: evil in a spiritual sense. If we are convinced about the existence of the devil, then we will see in him the ultimate personification of evil. But these examples are not all the same; not all are evil at the same level. Does evil exist? The answer must be yes; we will each recognise the concept of evil in at least one of the above examples, if not in all of them.

He Who Pulls the Strings

The New Testament writers describe the devil as the root cause of evil; Jesus himself referred to the devil, giving him the title 'the evil one'.[1] Clearly, he does epitomise evil, but not in the way that we might expect. The caricature devil that we looked at in the previous topic, the one with the horns, tail and trident, shows us a physical depiction of what we typically recognise as evil. But this is not a true picture. The devil is not a comic character; he is real and scheming and 'invisible'. That is to say that the devil works behind the scenes, pulling strings like a puppeteer. He brings about evil things in support of his purpose of spoiling what God has created. What is evil about the devil is that he stands in opposition to God. It is misleading to think of him as a demonic parody; the Bible tells us that he can sometimes appear as if an 'angel of light' – indeed he is an angelic being, a fallen angel.[2]

So far we have referred to different levels of evil behaviour, and have recognised that there are spiritual forces of evil led by the devil. We have also clarified that he is not a comical figure nor is he like the fearsome caricatures of horror films, but more akin to a single-minded, determined military opponent.[3]

Taking Sides

We recognise evil when we become aware that things are not good. We might say that being wasteful is an evil – it may entail being profligate with natural resources such as energy and causing unnecessary harm to the environment. We might see addiction to 'recreational' drugs as evil – this may result in antisocial behaviour, may degrade the person and their ability to contribute effectively to society, and will harm their mental and physical health. We may recognise paedophilia as evil – something that causes untold harm to the subjects of the abuse. We recognise this behaviour as unnatural and abusive of the innocent. But it also undermines the moral character of the perpetrator and saddles them with an enormous burden of guilt.

We may recognise acts of terrorism as evil – arbitrary acts that are aimed at causing indiscriminate harm and done for the purpose of making a point rather than securing a military advance. We may consider war crimes as evil – acting out of vengeance, delighting in causing unwarranted suffering and death. There are so many scenarios where we consider that evil acts occur, and we may view all of these as originating from moral corruption on the part of the perpetrator. Where this moral corruption is extreme, we may consider the actual person to be evil in themselves; someone amoral, incapable of conducting themselves in line with the behavioural norms of the wider society; someone who positively delights in acting destructively. When anyone does any of these things they are, maybe inadvertently, siding with the devil, because ultimately each of these things are done against God.

Getting Close to Home

The more we think about the nature of evil, the nearer we get to who we ourselves are. The illustrations above are probably extreme compared to our own behaviour, except perhaps for the first one about being wasteful. But there are many more examples of evil thoughts or behaviour that are much closer to home. All of these involve asserting ourselves, our wills and perceived self-interest over other people; whether we do this directly through individual defiance such as that of a wayward adolescent, or collectively through acts that break societies' laws. In the New Testament the apostle Paul quotes the writer in the Old Testament book of Psalms who states: "The fool says in his heart, 'There is no God.' They are corrupt, their deeds are vile; there is no one who does good."[4] He then goes on to declare: "for all have sinned and fall short of the glory of God."[5] We have all failed to meet the standard that God sets; we have all done things that we are ashamed of, things that could be classified as evil at one level or another. Thankfully Jesus has provided a way for our lives to be restored to God; for forgiveness for the sin and evil for which we are personally responsible.

Question 28 – Is there really a place called 'Hell'?

Carrot and Stick

There have been times when the Christian church has used the fear of hell as a means of frightening people into behaving the way that it was thought that they should; including frightening them into converting to Christianity. We might think of this in the context of the middle ages, but it has not been so uncommon in relatively modern times as well. We are probably all familiar with the concept of 'carrot and stick'; in this instance hell is the stick. Many Christians today have a sneaking feeling that the church places insufficient emphasis on hell, and they may be right. However, the term 'hell' is used very infrequently in the Bible, whereas references to heaven appear very often indeed.

Etymology of Hell

The English word 'hell' is used to translate both Hebrew and Greek words that appear in the original languages of the Bible. These words were used to describe a specific valley outside of the ancient city of Jerusalem. During part of the Old Testament period this place was notorious as the location of an idolatrous religious cult that worshipped the Canaanite god Molech. Here the people practiced human sacrifice, specifically throwing infants into a burning furnace. Later on, this same piece of land was used as the city rubbish dump; it was a place where corpses of criminals, dead animals, and all sorts of refuse were thrown to be destroyed by burning. From this we can understand that the term hell is linked in the Bible with a place associated with rebellion against God, a place where things of no use were disposed of, and a place where fire raged. Put together this encapsulates the biblical concept of hell rather well. Having seen where the term actually originates from, we still have to consider whether hell as we understand it actually exists.

A Hellish Place

Within the New Testament writings, nearly all of the instances of the term hell are directly associated with words spoken by Jesus: Jesus taught about hell. Accordingly, we must clearly recognise that the concept of hell has a central place within Christian understanding. The question that still remains is whether or not hell is an actual place, as such, in the spiritual realm. The answer would appear to be quite straightforward – if heaven is a place that represents the environment of God's presence, then it is logical to define hell as the environment where God is absent. That is to say, if heaven is a place, and if heaven is not everywhere, then hell must exist as a separate place.[1]

There has been a tendency to think of hell as a place of punishment – 'the fires of hell'. As a society we have little room for the concept of punishment for the sake of punishment. We are ok with the idea of punishment as a correctional measure; in the USA prisons are actually referred to as correctional institutions. We are also ok with the idea of incarcerating felons as a means of protecting society. But we in the UK no longer have corporal punishment and not many states in the USA continue to use the death penalty. So, what of hell? Is it a place of correction – are people assigned there temporarily in order to protect everyone else, or is it the ultimate place of punishment?

Raison D'être

One of the themes that reoccur in this book is that God is God. He is not 'one of us'. He is not like us. If we want to know reality and truth, then we need to look at what God has to tell us. We are greatly mistaken if we expect that God will fit in with our ideas. When it comes to knowing about hell from what we can learn from the Bible, then the only understanding that we can come to is that hell is indeed the ultimate place of punishment; it serves no other purpose. But, along with this understanding, we also need to appreciate that God is just. If we go to hell then this will be the direct and inevitable consequence of the choices that we have made.[2] If we choose to live our lives without God, effectively to live in rebellion against God, then when our lives on earth are over we can expect to continue in this same state. However, things aren't quite that simple.

Justice Prevailing

The Bible tells us that God is just.[3] Justice requires that there be a well-considered judgement; a decision needs to be made for every case. We are not assigned to hell directly because of our rejection of God, but because we have done wrong. It is most certainly true that everyone has done wrong. According to what we can read in the Bible, none of us lives up to God's standards.[4] The difference between those who choose to follow and obey God and those who choose otherwise is in relation to forgiveness. A Christian is a sinner like everyone else, but a forgiven sinner. Someone who does not choose God, and therefore does not ask for his forgiveness for the wrong that they have done, is a sinner who has not been forgiven. According to what we can learn from the Bible, we all have to face the judgement of God for the wrong that we have done.[5] The difference is that some have received forgiveness, which has 'washed the slate clean', while others have not, and therefore are required to bear the consequences.

Hell-Bent

What hell is actually like can only be guessed at – similarly to heaven. The Bible gives us indications but certainly not a full picture. It must surely be that the incompleteness of the picture indicates that we don't need to know exactly what hell is like. For most people it is sufficient to understand that hell is the destiny of all who reject Jesus Christ. Those who accept him and receive from God the forgiveness and new life that is available through Jesus' sacrifice have no need to know about hell. As for those who reject Jesus, they are by definition not interested in responding to God or the teaching of the Bible.

There is an expression that is still in common use today: 'hell-bent'. We refer to an individual being hell-bent on a particular course of action. This is used to mean someone who is determined to do their own thing, without regard for the likely consequences. We all know that there are consequences for every decision that we take, for our every action. This is both a scientific and a moral principle. Very often we are oblivious to the full effect of our choices; we may only see what is directly in front of us, the immediate objective. But there are also hidden consequences for ourselves and often for other people too. Many people are hell-bent – with little idea of their direction of travel.

❖ **Question 29 – Who is the Holy Spirit?**

The Third Person

Hopefully, before reading this topic you will have looked at the question in the Study section: 'What is meant by the "Trinity", and is this important?' (Q 9). If you haven't, then it will be helpful to take a look before continuing here.

The Trinity is the Christian teaching about the nature of God. Christians recognise one God, but in three distinct persons; God the Father, God the Son (Jesus), and God the Holy Spirit. The first thing to appreciate from this is that the Holy Spirit is God in just the same way as the Father is God and the Son is God. Secondly, the Holy Spirit is a person; he is often referred to as the third person of the Trinity. Sadly, some people do not appreciate this and so refer to him as 'it' – the Holy Spirit is a person and deserves the personal pronoun 'he'.[1] This misunderstanding is something that has been engendered by the old King James version of the Bible, where instead of 'Holy Spirit' the term 'Holy Ghost' was misleadingly used in translation; we don't tend to think of ghosts as persons!

A Comforter

For many religious people, the Holy Spirit has a low profile; he is more like a nodding acquaintance than an intimate friend. This is quite different to how he is referred to in the New Testament writings. After Jesus was raised from the dead he promised that he would ask the Father to send the Holy Spirit. Jesus himself was going to return to his Father in heaven, but the Holy Spirit was to come to Jesus' followers and be the representative of God to them:

> But the Advocate, the Holy Spirit, whom the Father will send in my name, will teach you all things and will remind you of everything I have said to you.[2]

In this verse from the Gospel according to John, the word 'Advocate' is used to translate the original Greek word that means 'Comforter', meaning one who gives support. This ministry of the Holy Spirit is very important but is not the full extent of his role – far from it. As well as giving comfort and support, the Holy Spirit imbues Christians with power from God. Before Jesus returned to his Father in heaven, he promised:

> But you will receive power when the Holy Spirit comes on you; and you will be my witnesses in Jerusalem, and in all Judea and Samaria, and to the ends of the earth.[3]

Special Gifts

At the time, Jesus' followers didn't really understand what the promise of the Holy Spirit would mean. But they soon discovered that God the Holy Spirit was going to be with them and would work powerfully through them. This was evident from the time that the Holy Spirit came upon the first followers of Jesus – see the Dining Room topic: 'What does it mean to be a Pentecostal Christian?' (Q 46). They were empowered with boldness from God and, of equal importance, with spiritual gifts and abilities. There are a number of different spiritual gifts that are mentioned in the New Testament books, among these are the power to work miracles and to heal people in Jesus' name, to have hidden truth revealed, and also to receive prophetic words from God that reveal his purposes.[4] These gifts are given by the Holy Spirit to different Christians, according to how God chooses to work through each person; they are gifts for the church as a whole that are entrusted to different individuals.[5]

Strange Mystical Power?

For someone who is not yet a Christian, the idea that God would live with them, empower them and also imbue them with special gifts and abilities, will probably seem 'other worldly'. This is why this topic about the Holy Spirit has been placed within the TV Room. It is important to emphasise, however, that the Holy Spirit is not some strange mystical power; he is a person, and he is God. It has been said that the Holy Spirit is a gentleman – he doesn't push into the lives of Christians but waits to be invited. Above all, he is the Comforter who is involved in the lives of Christians to help them, reassure them and strengthen them.

Emotional Crutch?

This all goes to emphasise that genuine Christian faith is not a fantasy, an 'emotional crutch' as some have characterised it. The message of the Bible, from start to finish, is that there are spiritual realities that we are generally unaware of. We tend to go about our daily lives oblivious to what is occurring in the spiritual realm, whether it is the work of God or of sinister forces. God knows that if Christians are to stand for him, and if they are to reach out to other people with the message of his love, his forgiveness and his kingdom, then they cannot do this spiritual work with mere human resources. Christians need spiritual resources; they rely on the power that the Holy Spirit gives.

Question 30 – Does God heal today?

Something New?

The idea of God restoring people to health is nothing new and wasn't even a new concept when Jesus started to minister. Healing is evident throughout the Bible, where numerous instances are documented, both within the Old and the New Testaments. Often this is physical healing, but there are also instances of people being set free from spiritual oppression. It was in large part Jesus' healing ministry that attracted people to follow him and to listen to what he taught.[1] One might imagine that healing would cease after Jesus' time on earth, but this is definitely not the case. The end of the four gospels (which are the accounts of the life of Jesus) does not mark the end of healing within the New Testament. In fact, very early in the next book (the Acts of the Apostles) we see Jesus' followers ministering healing in a dramatic way. A very public healing caused quite a stir amongst the people in the surrounding area.[2]

Power from God

Many who understand about Jesus will not be surprised that he was able to heal people, but they may be less certain about other people ministering healing, as recorded in the New Testament. These 'other people' were in themselves very ordinary men; what made them different was the fact that they had spent time with Jesus. We see that this point was not lost on the religious leaders of the day:

> When they saw the courage of Peter and John and realised that they were unschooled, ordinary men, they were astonished and they took note that these men had been with Jesus.[3]

During his time on earth, Jesus had sent out his followers to do their own work of ministry. He instructed them to: "Heal those who are ill, raise the dead, cleanse those who have leprosy, drive out demons."[4] So it is perhaps not so strange that this ministry would continue after Jesus left them. However, the New Testament writers give no indication that this did happen again until after the coming of the Holy Spirit – see the previous topic. It is the coming of the Holy Spirit that was crucial for the ongoing ministry of healing after the time of Jesus, and it is also the Holy Spirit who is crucial for the healing ministry of the church today. This is because healing is a spiritual ministry, which can only be undertaken through the power that God gives. The coming of the Holy Spirit was to give God's people the power and spiritual gifting to minister. In his first letter to the Corinthians, the apostle Paul explains how the Holy Spirit gives spiritual gifts to Christians, including the gift of healing.[5]

Rediscovering Normality

We see numerous instances of healing recorded in the Acts of the Apostles. But we also see from the New Testament letters that healing was considered a normal part of Christian ministry. This brings us back to the question about whether God heals today.

Although the church has never quite lost the expectation of healing, over the last five decades or so there has been a renewed focus on the topic. That is because this period coincides with Christians having become more aware of the ministry of the Holy Spirit. It was the realisation that Christians are supposed to have spiritual power from God that brought about this relatively recent change. This realisation was that the powerful ministry we read about happening in the New Testament is also meant for Christians today. Even now there are Christians who do not accept this, but who believe that this ministry was isolated to the time immediately following the period when Jesus lived on earth. Obviously, it is very sad if people ignore what God is still doing through his church, but it is also immaterial in the light of experience. Just as there are millions of Christians alive today who have experienced the power of the Holy Spirit in their lives, there are also very many who can testify to the power of God to heal today. The simple answer to the question "Does God heal today?" is that, yes, he does.

Let's be Cautious

Rather than simply leaving the question at this point, it is important to inject a note of caution. Healing is something of a hot topic. It is something that we look for because so many people are in need of healing, and for each one their ailments are a big issue. This applies both to committed Christians and to those who are not yet Christian. Many churches are enthusiastic to see God heal. Individual Christians who have already experienced the power of God healing people, want to see more individuals restored to health and fitness through the power that he gives. There are, however, some religious groups, and individuals, who have an unbalanced understanding of how God ministers healing. These sometimes claim that healing has occurred when it has not. In making false or exaggerated claims these people cause real harm to the sufferers involved, while at the same time bringing dishonour to God. We have to conclude that healing of all types does occur today through the authority of Jesus, and by the power of the Holy Spirit, but this isn't an 'on-demand' process. God heals today when his followers honour him and listen to his voice.

❖ Question 31 – What does a relationship with God look like?

Inside Out

'What does that look like' is an expression that is commonly used when we want to talk about the impact of an idea – moving from the theoretical or philosophical to the tangible outworking of something. In this instance the term 'look like' could be misleading, as though the outworking of a relationship with God is something physical or outward. In reality this relationship is hidden, and its outworking is a change on the inside of the person. That said, it is often the inner change that people notice when someone becomes a Christian and embarks upon a relationship with God; the onlooker sees this change revealed through the person's demeanour and behaviour.

Quick Win

There are two things that most people experience when they become a Christian. The first is a very clear sense of freedom from the burden of guilt and shame, and from what the Bible terms 'sin'. This is because they become deeply conscious of having received forgiveness from God – having their 'slate wiped clean'. This forgiveness was promised in the Old Testament where we read:

> He has removed our sins as far away from us as the east is from the west.[1]

> Though your sins are like scarlet, they shall be as white as snow; though they are red as crimson, they shall be like wool.[2]

In the classic spiritual allegory *The Pilgrim's Progress*, sin is depicted as something akin to a very heavy rucksack. Christian, the main character, is burdened with carrying this load everywhere he goes, until he receives forgiveness from God, at which point it falls away and he is no longer weighed down – he is freed from his burden.

Directions

The second experience for new Christians is that they become aware of having a relationship with God. Previously they were estranged from God, but now relationship is restored. It is a relationship based on love: God's love for them, and their response to that love. As part of becoming a Christian, we are forgiven for the wrong things that have been done in the past, and also God gives guidance for the future. This means that Christians seek to live to please God – to live the way that he shows them, and to accept his direction in their decisions and choices. It simply doesn't make sense to ask God for forgiveness, only to continue doing whatever we like and thereby continuing to make bad choices. What does make sense is to recognise our need of direction, and to ask God to show us how to live the best way, the way that will be pleasing to him. This is like a coin with two sides: forgiveness for the past and direction for the future. It would be very sad if the coin had only one of these sides: forgiveness but no help to change our lives, or change in direction but no clearing of our 'debt' for the wrong things that we have done in the past.

Something Different

There are different ways in which God guides Christians, but the most important is simply through them knowing him. To know God means that their consciences become sensitised to what pleases him and what hurts him. This isn't about following rules or religious practices.

Most Christians want to tell other people about God's love and forgiveness, but often there isn't an appropriate opportunity to actually explain about Christian faith. However, other people generally appreciate that there is something different about a Christian, maybe not through what they say, or through what they may have been told about the person, but rather through who they are. This might be because the Christian avoids using bad language or doesn't partake in gossip; or maybe because they are more patient, positive or generous-hearted than other people tend to be. Whatever the reason, people seem to sense that there is something different about someone who is a Christian.

Having a relationship with God operates in a similar way. A Christian may not have been taught that certain behaviour is wrong, but they can sense in their spirit when they are doing things that are not pleasing to God. Whilst Christians have this relationship with God, they nonetheless have freewill and still have decisions to make. Christians still need to make the choice to do what pleases God.

Good Practice

There are various things that Christians choose to do in order to know God better and to understand how he wants them to live their lives. They pray regularly, conversing with God and sharing their thoughts with him. They also spend time listening to what God may have to tell them. Most Christians also take the opportunity to read from the Bible regularly. This is because the Bible is a great source of information about how God wants people to live[3] – it has been referred to as the 'user's manual' for the Christian. Christians usually also choose to meet together regularly, both for formal times of worship and learning, and informal times for sharing their lives together. All of these things are there to help Christians to understand God's purposes and how to live the way that he wants for them, the way that enables him to bless them.

Starting Over

The thing about a relationship with God is that it is life-changing. When someone embarks upon this relationship through asking God to forgive them, and asking him to lead their lives, they start to change – from the inside out. It is very clear from the Bible that God is interested in what goes on inside a person much more than outside.[4] He knows that the external reflects what is happening on the inside, and it is the inside that needs to change. This is the place where God the Holy Spirit works, starting with the cleansing that comes from forgiveness for everything that has gone before, and continuing through the renewal of the person's motivation and thinking.[5]

Question 32 – How can we know what God is saying to us?

Hearing from God

Whole new religious belief systems have been based on what individuals claim that they have heard God tell them or reveal to them. Many people claim to hear God, and so it is understandable that we feel very cautious if someone says that God has spoken to them.

Indeed, we are correct in being cautious, even sceptical. However, we need to balance this reservation with the fact that we actually do want to hear from God, and he does actually speak to people in a variety of ways.

Gentle Whisper

Someone who is not yet a Christian, but who recognises their need for a relationship with God will want to hear from him; they won't be content to make a spiritual commitment based on hearsay but need to be deeply convinced that he is real. The person who has started to have a relationship with God wants to hear from him; they seek ongoing direction and guidance, they want to become familiar with the 'sound of his voice' so that they can recognise him when he speaks to them. Most of all, God himself wants to speak with us, to reveal himself to us, and he will do so if we have sincere, open hearts. The thing is that he rarely shouts; his voice is usually very soft and gentle. In the Old Testament there is a story concerning the prophet Elijah and an encounter that he had with God, who promised that he would pass by in front of Elijah. We read:

> Then a great and powerful wind tore the mountains apart and shattered the rocks before the Lord, but the Lord was not in the wind. After the wind there was an earthquake, but the Lord was not in the earthquake. After the earthquake came a fire, but the Lord was not in the fire. And after the fire came a gentle whisper.[1]

Elijah recognised the voice of God in that gentle whisper, and this is how we should expect that God will speak to us; our difficulty is in recognising his voice.

Listening and Hearing

There are different ways in which God speaks to us. In my own experience there have been only two occasions where I have been aware of him speaking to me with a message in what I sensed to be audible words. Both times there was just one single word, but there was no uncertainty in my mind as to what it was that God was telling me. Usually when God is speaking we don't receive actual words as such, but have a sense of what he is saying, like a realisation or revelation. We would all prefer it if God spoke more loudly, more definitely and clearly, but this isn't his way. God speaks to those who are willing to hear, to those who are actively listening.

We should also appreciate that God normally reveals things to us by less direct means than speaking. We can be convinced that we are hearing God through reading the Bible, or through reading, or listening to, Christian teaching. We can also hear God through the conversations that we have with other people. Even before we become Christians, there is a way in which we can hear God: by being convinced about the truth of the Christian message of forgiveness. We may read about this message or be told about it. We may look into the Bible to check that it is really written there. We may talk to people who are already Christians to help us understand what God's forgiveness means in practice. But in the end, however solid the proposition appears to be, we need to be convinced that God is for real before we are in a position to act upon what we conclude to be true. This is where we need to hear God speaking, assuring us of his love and purposes for us. It is important to know that if we seek the truth, then God will reveal it to us; he loves us and is not slow to tell us if we are willing to hear him.[2]

The Touchstone

We began this topic by recognising that people can mistakenly think that they have heard from God when this isn't really the case. So, we should consider how we can know that it is really God that we have been hearing. After all it could be just our own thoughts, based on our imaginations or emotions; or else it could be an ungodly spiritual influence that has sought to mislead us. A Christian who is accustomed to hearing God will be used to his 'voice' and be able to recognise what is from God and what is not. But for others there is a greater reliance upon external validation. One method that is available to us is to check that what we think we have received from God is consistent with what we can find written in the Bible. Anything that is from God will be in harmony with the Bible, which is the touchstone – God will never reveal anything to us that is at odds with Bible truth.

Is that You God?

There is a second means that we may have available to us to check out what we feel that God is saying, which is to submit those thoughts to other people who know God. This might be a leader in the church or someone who we respect and trust, who has been a Christian for some time. The important thing is that the other person is trustworthy. The benefit of submitting to godly people is that they can 'weigh' what we believe we have heard from God. Then they will either encourage us and help us if God is indeed speaking to us or warn us and explain why our thoughts are not consistent with how God is. This is a win-win situation – if we are sincere about seeking truth then there is nothing to lose. We will get encouragement in what is actually true, or else the untrue will be unmasked, and we will be duly warned that it is not from God after all. In the latter case we will probably be helped to understand how God speaks and be encouraged to continue listening for his voice.

Hearing God is a difficult area because God only speaks to us on his own terms. Often we want to hear, but on our terms – and this doesn't work out at all well. God will speak to a Christian who is open and sincere, and what he says will be for their good.

Question 33 – Is there really going to be a 'second coming' of Jesus?

Big News

Within the newspaper industry there is something known as 'second coming' type, which is a huge typeface that is used for only the most extreme and dramatic headlines. This font gets its name from an event that hasn't even occurred yet, but which will undoubtedly be the biggest news ever. This event is the second coming of Jesus Christ.

It's No Joke

You may be confused at this point, wondering what is meant by a 'second coming of Jesus'. This is something that is directly foretold within the New Testament writings, including by Jesus himself as recorded in the Gospel according to John.[1] At the beginning of the next book, the Acts of the Apostles, we are told how Jesus was taken up into heaven at the end of his earthly ministry. This account goes on to tell us that the disciples of Jesus who watched this event were met by angels who had a message for them.[2] This message was that Jesus will return one day in just the same way that they witnessed his ascent into heaven. The promise of Jesus' return has been held onto by the church ever since – a second coming of Jesus to mankind. This is fundamental Christian teaching, something that all orthodox Christians accept and believe.

Anticipation

A long time has passed since this promise was made, and at different points in history there has been renewed emphasis on the expectation of Jesus' return. This is most often because the church has found itself under pressure of one sort or another, starting with the persecution of Christians in the early centuries after the time of Jesus. While the Bible is clear about the return of Jesus, it is very much less clear about exactly what this will mean and is decidedly unclear about when it will happen. In fact, Jesus told his disciples that neither he himself nor the angels in heaven knew when his return would take place.[3] There have been occasions when various pseudo-Christian sects have falsely declared that Jesus has already returned;

in reality we are still awaiting his return. There are various signs that are indicated in the books of the Bible, things that we are told must occur before Jesus will come back. Some Christians interpret world circumstances in the light of these Bible indicators, suggesting that the return of Jesus is imminent. But the truth is that nobody can know. All that we can do is to be prepared for when that day does come – it may be tomorrow, next month, next year or in the more distant future.

Dubious Interpretations

It is now time for a note of caution: there are people who make a big thing about what is commonly referred to as the 'end times' – the time surrounding the return of Jesus, and what will happen before, during and after that event. These people are convinced that they understand in detail what will occur, how it will occur and even when it will occur. These 'end times' gurus expend a great deal of effort teaching their beliefs and trying to convince others that their interpretations are correct. It is true that the Bible writers do give us hints and indications, but that is all that we can glean. We cannot know anything for sure except that we have the promise that one day Jesus will return, and that we should both look forward to, and be prepared for, that day.

Second Chance?

For someone who is not yet a Christian, the teaching of the Bible about the return of Jesus is important to note. Every topic covered in this book is to do with spiritual realities, opening our eyes to God's purposes for mankind and for each of us as individuals. The return of Jesus is clearly promised – we all need to decide whether or not we believe in this promise, and to live our lives accordingly. The coming of Jesus in the first place had been promised for a very long time and was looked forward to by God's people. The problem was that most of these people refused to recognise him when he did come; many of their descendants still don't accept Jesus. When Jesus comes for the second time there will be no mistaking who he is.

Something else that we should know is that the purpose of the second coming of Jesus is very different to that of his first coming. Jesus came to live and die for mankind – to teach God's ways and to die in our place so that we can ask for, and receive, forgiveness from God. When Jesus comes the second time it will not be to preach or to teach, neither will it be to give people a second chance to accept him. It is now, today, that we have the opportunity to accept Jesus – his second coming marks an end to this opportunity. When Jesus comes again it will be to gather those who are his people, who have already asked God for forgiveness and have been living for him.[4]

The Kitchen

Question 34 – Are the Ten Commandments applicable to Christians today?

Tablets of Stone

According to the Bible, the Ten Commandments were given by God to his people, the Jews, after their escape from the Egyptian Pharaoh. We see in the Bible that God himself inscribed the words of the Commandments onto two stone tablets.[1] Although the Ten Commandments are often thought of as 'laws' or 'rules', these terms don't adequately describe their status for the people of God in Old Testament times. The commandments were an integral part of a covenant-based relationship between God and the nation he had chosen as his own.[2]

As many people are unfamiliar with what the Ten Commandments actually state, it is helpful to list them.[3] So here we go:

1. You shall have no other gods before me.

2. You shall not make for yourself an image in the form of anything in heaven above or on the earth beneath or in the waters below. You shall not bow down to them or worship them; for I, the Lord your God, am a jealous God, punishing the children for the sin of the parents to the third and fourth generation of those who hate me, but showing love to a thousand generations of those who love me and keep my commandments.

3. You shall not misuse the name of the Lord your God, for the Lord will not hold anyone guiltless who misuses his name.

4. Remember the Sabbath day by keeping it holy. Six days you shall labour and do all your work, but the seventh day is a sabbath to the Lord your God. On it you shall not do any work, neither you, nor your son or daughter, nor your male or female servant, nor your animals, nor any foreigner residing in your towns. For in six days the Lord made the heavens and the earth, the sea, and all that is in them, but he rested on the seventh day. Therefore the Lord blessed

the Sabbath day and made it holy.

5. Honour your father and your mother, so that you may live long in the land the Lord your God is giving you.

6. You shall not murder.

7. You shall not commit adultery.

8. You shall not steal.

9. You shall not give false testimony against your neighbour.

10. You shall not covet your neighbour's house. You shall not covet your neighbour's wife, or his male or female servant, his ox or donkey, or anything that belongs to your neighbour.

It goes without saying that the Commandments were couched in terms that were appropriate for the people who initially received them; there are references to servant, ox and donkey that don't apply to most people in the Western world today. However this doesn't change the meaning of the Commandments – we are all able to mentally update these terms to relate to our own culture and environment.

A Rules Game?

Traditionally, churches have tended to view the Ten Commandments as 'rules' that should still be followed, which is something that could be inferred from Jesus' own reference to them in the gospel accounts. However, the Christian faith is very different to Old Testament Jewish faith, which entailed close observance of rules. The essential difference is that Christian faith is not based on following a set of rules but on a direct relationship with God; this relationship was made possible through the death of Jesus. Accordingly, many Christians today are reluctant to see the Ten Commandments as a set of rules that are directly binding upon them. This is not because they think them to be wrong in any way, but because they know that following a rules-based code of behaviour is not a basis for pleasing God.

Raised Eyebrows

People generally agree that most, if not all, of the Ten Commandments are good and right, to the extent of questioning the faith of anyone who claims to be a Christian but does not follow these 'rules'. There are, however, a few of the commandments that may cause raised eyebrows, and it would be helpful to look at these briefly.

Image Makers

The second commandment refers to the making of images of living things – photographers beware! Not really. The focus of this commandment relates to worshipping such images, rather than making them. In the culture of early Old Testament times the only reason for making images was to use them as a focus of religious observance. Our world today is awash with images of one sort or another, but very rarely are these used for religious worship.

A Special Day?

The fourth commandment, to observe the Sabbath day, is probably the most contentious of the ten; the difficulty with it might even be seen as a modern issue due to changes in society. It is not so very long ago that Sunday was generally recognised as a day of rest and was understood to be a Sabbath. But the world has changed such that keeping a day separate and different from the others is now much harder to achieve, even for those who sincerely wish to do so. Some will quite rightly argue that the Sabbath referred to in the Ten Commandments is actually the seventh day of the week, which is Saturday rather than Sunday. The move to Sunday was an adjustment that the first Christians chose to make, partly because they wanted to honour God with the first day of the week (Sunday) rather than the last day, but also because it was on a Sunday that Jesus rose from the dead.

A Revolutionary Idea

I remember reading that during the days of the French revolution the revolutionary authorities decided that the week should consist of ten days rather than seven, with just one in ten being a day of rest. The French gave this a good try, but it wasn't very long before this project was dropped. The thing is that the people struggled with a system that gave only one day of rest in ten. This highlights for us the fact that we actually need to take a day of rest – one day in seven. This is a fundamental principle that was encapsulated within the Ten Commandments that God provided for his people to follow.

This one is Tough

The fifth commandment – to 'honour your father and your mother' – is a hard one to comply with, and one that some will baulk at. The essential premise for this commandment is that our parents want the best for us, and that they know us rather well, in some respects perhaps even better than we know ourselves. Therefore, it makes good sense to respect them and to acknowledge that they have views that are worthy of careful consideration. We all know, however, that just as we are not perfect, the same applies to our parents; some people have parents who do not in themselves merit much respect.

People of Principle

Getting back to the question, we must surely acknowledge that the commandments are intended for our benefit. They need to be understood in context, but they also need to be taken seriously – all of them.[4] For the Christian, the very fact that God himself gave these Ten Commandments is sufficient reason for them to be taken seriously, not as rigid rules, but as God-given principles for his people to follow.[5]

Question 35 – Why don't Christians adhere to the laws in the Old Testament?

The Leviticus Challenge

We have already looked at the Ten Commandments, but there are a great many more rules that the Jewish people of the Old Testament were required to obey. These rules are outlined within the first five books of the Bible, but especially in the third of these, the book known as 'Leviticus'. Most people find this to be a challenging book, in part because it outlines, in sometimes tedious detail, various rules for healthy living. Another difficulty with the rules in Leviticus is that they don't immediately appear relevant to us today. There are definitely lessons that we can learn from this book however, some which modern man has only come to appreciate the importance of in relatively recent times. For instance, 19th century hospitals were incredibly dangerous places for patients due to the likelihood of contracting infections; had the medics of the day observed the hygiene rules outlined in Leviticus then countless lives would have been spared, and enormous suffering avoided.

What's it all About

The rules for right living outlined in the Old Testament were there for different purposes:

1. To protect the people from things that would harm them physically: infections, illnesses, etc.

2. To encourage people to deal with each other fairly; in particular, rules related to the poor and to those in need.

3. To provide a code for the administration of justice.

4. To protect women and children from abuse.

5. To steer people away from moral corruption.

6. To steer people away from corruption in their worship of God.

7. To ensure that the people knew how God required them to worship him.

Making things Worse

We are thinking about rules that are recorded within the Old Testament writings, but it is worth mentioning that the Jewish teachers in Old Testament times went on to elaborate upon these rules. Their intention was to provide interpretation with a view to clarification, but the effect of this effort was to make the rules very complex, hard to understand and even harder to follow. In the Gospel according to Matthew, in the New Testament, we find that Jesus was critical of the Jewish teachers for this. They were emphasising the details of their rules but missing the more important matters of God's law: justice, mercy and faithfulness.[1]

Principles vs. Stipulations

Christians value the Old Testament, including the difficult book of Leviticus, but are not bound to follow the rules outlined there. For instance, there were strict rules about what kind of meat it was acceptable to eat. Many people are aware that even today observers of the Jewish faith are forbidden to eat pork. However, Christians are not bound by such restrictions. It must again be emphasised that Christian faith is not based on the observance of particular rules; rather, acceptance by God is based on what Jesus achieved for us when he died on the cross. This is not to suggest that Christian faith has no rules, but that Christians are guided by principles rather than stipulations.[2] As with the case of the hygiene rules that were mentioned earlier, much of the guidance within the Old Testament is still very pertinent for us today, and is ignored at our peril. The New Testament writers point out that we need to grasp the principles behind these rules, and then to take these to heart. But at the same time, we should avoid trying to slavishly observe a set of rules whatever merit these may have, somehow imagining that such observance could earn credit with God.

Question 36 – The God of the Bible seems harsh - is he really like that?

The Big Picture

There are some passages in the Bible that, at first reading, can lead us to think that God is rather harsh. These mainly appear within the Old Testament, but not exclusively so. As with many of the topics that are discussed in this book, it is essential that we look not only at the details, but also the bigger picture. And if we truly want to understand why certain things have happened, then we need to see what lies behind the details as well. It is often possible to do this simply by reading the chapters before and after any particular Bible story. This gives context, which is an essential ingredient for understanding anything that we might read in the Bible.

What does 'Holy' mean?

If we consider the Bible in its entirety, then there are two things that it is hard to miss. The first is God's unfathomable love, deep compassion and great patience; the second is that God is God! We tend to refer to him as being holy. When used in relation to God the term 'holy' relates to moral excellence and uncompromised perfection. This is the nature of God – if we choose to honour him then this is the nature of the God we honour. We are not like God, and sometimes struggle with Bible passages that display the holiness of God.

Corporate Responsibility

We find it hard when we read of God's punishment of groups of people in the Bible. We don't fully appreciate why he has done this. Actually, we can be quite inconsistent about this because, at other times, we question why God doesn't appear to intervene in circumstances that we consider terrible today. We ask: "Why does God allow this?" These are indeed difficult questions, and ultimately we need to appreciate that God's perspective is different to ours; he sees the whole picture, and he always does what is right. Some say that accepting this is an act of faith; I prefer to use the term 'trust'. The ultimate question is whether or not we are willing to trust God. Are we willing to recognise that he will always do what is morally right, based on his complete understanding of every circumstance? We of course are not morally perfect, and never have a full understanding of any circumstance, so we are in no position to sit in judgment upon God's actions. My wife, Jean, occasionally talks to God along the lines of: "If I were you I wouldn't do it that way God; but I am grateful that you know better than I do, and I trust you to always do what is right."

Choices

The bottom line is that each of us is responsible for our own actions and also for their consequences. We may feel that we have done some wrong things in innocence, but most of us can recognise, most of the time, that our wrong acts are the result of our deliberate choices. We may choose to view any resultant consequences, or punishment, as unfair, but if we step back and consider the turn of events soberly, then we can appreciate that the consequences were just. This is a bit like the law breaker who is caught in the act of committing the crime, who declares to the police officer: "it's a fair cop." He recognises that he has done wrong, accepts the arrest, and knows that he probably deserves the punishment that will inevitably be handed down by the magistrate or judge.

Some people really struggle when they see in the Bible that God's punishment was administered at a corporate level.[1] There are occasions when families, peoples or nations were held accountable and everyone shared the consequences. This type of accountability is quite foreign to most of us today, but it was familiar to the people who lived in Old Testament times; it was the norm. There was an understanding of shared guilt, shared responsibility and shared consequences.

A New Paradigm

We can all think of circumstances where the many have been punished for the acts of the few – for instance when the school class is punished for the misdemeanour of one or two classmates. Is that unfair? Actually, most of us would say that it is. But this isn't what we see acted out in those difficult Old Testament stories; here there are corporate consequences due to corporate wrongdoing. Although the wrongdoing may not have been participated in by absolutely everyone, there was a principle of corporate responsibility.

Corporate responsibility also encompassed family responsibility, with offspring paying the price for the wrongdoing of parents. This was the normal pattern in those days, but that was going to change. We can see in the Old Testament prophetic book of Jeremiah a promise from God that a time was coming when each person would be held to account for their own wrongdoings, rather than having to suffer because of the sins of their parents.[2] Now that we live in that time, we struggle to appreciate how things worked previously.

Question 37 – Are there any rules associated with being a Christian?

Misleading?

Christian faith is not based on rules but on the attitude of peoples' hearts. This is fundamentally different to that of the Jewish religion, as outlined in the Old Testament. The Old Testament stipulates an extensive range of rules or laws that are to be followed, including the Ten Commandments, whereas there are no regulations associated with being a Christian. However, this statement is capable of being misunderstood. Whilst Christians are not bound by regulations, they are guided by spiritual principles which relate to the whole of life and which represent a more comprehensive framework that any rule book could ever provide.

A Tick in the Box?

James, in his New Testament letter, explains that it is not sufficient to say that we have faith; true faith must be revealed in our actions as well. James tells us that faith without actions is actually dead.[1] What we really believe is evidenced not by what we say but by what we do. When it comes to 'rules' (or laws), James writes:

> If you really keep the royal law found in Scripture, 'Love your neighbour as yourself,' you are doing right.[2]

Here James is quoting one of God's commands, recorded in the Old Testament book of Leviticus. This being the case, we can certainly say that this is a rule that applies to Christians today, and not only to the Jewish people of the Old Testament times. However, it is couched as a general principle, rather than a 'tick in the box' type of rule to which we are able to say "yes, done that" and walk away. What we read about the life of Jesus shows us how he lived by this principle.

Real Life Illustration

Jesus was dedicated to obeying God. This dedication came to a climax when he gave up his life for everyone else – he did for us what we couldn't do for ourselves, something that he alone was qualified to do. In fact, when Jesus was asked what the greatest commandment is in the Old Testament law, he quoted the command of God about loving your neighbour. Actually, Jesus answered the question by quoting two laws: before loving our neighbour another law takes precedence:

> Love the Lord your God with all your heart and with all your soul and with all your strength and with all your mind.[3]

Jesus made it plain that these two principles form the basis upon which his followers should live their lives.

We need to consider how these two principles work out in practice in the life of a Christian today. The starting point is to recognise that whilst they have received God's forgiveness for the wrong things that they have done, this doesn't make Christians perfect – it simply means that they have been 'forgiven'. Our frail human nature causes us to be inherently selfish; becoming a Christian does not, in itself, change this. However, if Christians will allow him, then God will graciously work in their hearts over time to change how they think and feel.[4] As this work progresses their lives will better reflect how he wants them to be.

This need for Christians to be changed relates to both of the laws that Jesus quoted. Both require a deep change of heart from how we naturally and instinctively behave. It should also be noted that obedience to the second law is predicated upon taking the first to heart. If I don't love God and commit myself fully to living for him, then I will never have his heart for other people and love them in the way that he does – as reflected by Jesus' own life.

Who and How?

Let's conclude by briefly thinking about what 'loving our neighbour as ourselves' means in practice. After Jesus quoted this command of God, someone asked him the question 'who is my neighbour?' Jesus responded by telling a story – one of the best known of his illustrations – the parable of the Good Samaritan.[5] In this parable Jesus is explaining that 'neighbour' means anyone who we come across, whether they are like us or not. The obvious follow-on question for us has to be: "What does it mean to love your neighbour?" The answer is there in the Bible quotation, where it says to love your neighbour "as you love yourself". It is not appropriate here to go into depth about what this means in practice, but there is a point that it would be right to make. This quotation isn't saying that Christians should be at the beck and call of other people; that they have to do whatever other people might want them to (ie. to be a 'doormat'). The clue would seem to be in the words "love ... as you love yourself." In other words, be prepared to help meet other people's real needs, which might be quite different to their 'wants'.

A Stunning Example

There is a story in the New Testament book of the Acts of the Apostles that illustrates this very well. Two of Jesus' apostles were on their way to worship God when they came across a crippled man who was lying on the pavement begging for money; he had resorted to this because his disability meant that he had no means of actually earning a living. This man asked them to give him some money, which they did not do, but neither did they simply walk past and ignore him. Instead of the money that he asked for, they gave him something much more valuable – meeting his real need. The apostle Peter commanded the man, in the name of Jesus, to stand up and walk. The Bible story continues: "Taking him by the right hand, he helped him up, and instantly the man's feet and ankles became strong. He jumped to his feet and began to walk. Then he went with them into the temple courts, walking and jumping, and praising God."[6] We can see that rather than meeting a very transitory, felt need, the man's real need was met – the need for healing and restoration.

This is God's heart for each one of us; he wants to meet our real need. And this starts by meeting the deepest need of all which is to relieve us of our burden of guilt and shame, and to restore our relationship with himself.

❖ Question 38 – Do Christians have to obey God?

Expressing Love

Within the Bible writings, love for God and obedience to God are inextricably linked; obedience is shown as the response of love.[1] Loving God is essentially what being a Christian is all about. When anyone becomes a Christian there are enormous benefits that they receive themselves, but their choice is primarily an expression of love for God. The decision to become a Christian is an act of love, and in this very act they are worshipping God. We worship God whenever we recognise and acknowledge him for who he is. The reason why Christians go to great lengths to tell other people about God's love is so that these people may recognise him for who he is, and that they may themselves choose to love him, to worship him and obey him.

Insurance

The Christian message is that a relationship with God is for today, not for tomorrow only. In times past there may have been a tendency to try to frighten people into worshipping God, focussing on the reality of eternal punishment for sin. This approach is very sad because it tries to drive behaviour through fear instead of through love. Not only that, but it inherently means that only a part of the message is told. By this shrunken message, becoming a Christian appears to be like an insurance policy, or a get-out-of-jail-free card for when they die. The reality is quite different. Becoming a Christian is something that we do with our lives now. It just happens that this act also has ramifications for our eternal future.

Partnership

Even today many people make the decision to become Christians because they are acutely aware of their need for God's forgiveness, but then don't appreciate that the other side of the coin is that God wants, and offers, to partner with them on the journey through life. It is in this context that the idea of obedience to God comes in. When someone becomes a Christian this involves not only recognition of their wrongdoing – their sinfulness – but also recognition of their need for help to live in a way that pleases God. Anyone who loves God will want to live to please him and to fulfil his purpose for them. This means opening their hearts and lives to him. It means committing themselves to following the spiritual principles that were recorded by the writers of the New Testament. It also means responding to God whenever they sense that he has something specific to say to them personally. Does this amount to obedience? Yes it does, but it is obedience motivated by love rather than compliance with a set of stipulations.

The Journey

The current question asks whether Christians have to obey God. The answer is that, strictly, no they don't. In fact it is difficult to imagine anyone, who is not deluded, claiming that they do obey God in every respect all of the time.[2] We are all flawed human beings.[3] Becoming a Christian doesn't change this as if by waving a magic wand. When someone becomes a Christian they are freed from the burden of guilt and shame that results from the wrong things that they have done and thought. But it also opens the way to start afresh in a new life lived with, and for, God. This new way of living is a gradual process. They gradually learn that God is to be trusted in all of the circumstances of life. They gradually learn that what the Bible writers tell us is actually true and from God. They gradually learn that it is a mistake to ignore what God has to say. The result should be a growing conformity to living in the way that pleases God.[4] Obedience to God may be a decision that they make up front, but they need to work this out in experience – this is a journey.

Jail Time

It is said that the second most well-known book after the Bible is *The Pilgrim's Progress*, an allegorical tale written in 1678 by John Bunyan. The main storyline is of a Christian's journey through life from the time before he became a Christian to his entrance into the heavenly city. The book illustrates the highs and lows, the temptations and failures, as well as the moments of delight and exultation in a Christian's life. It is important to note that Bunyan began writing this work during a 12-year incarceration in Bedford jail. He wasn't there because he was bad, but because he chose to follow his conscience and preach about God openly at a time when the law placed restrictions on people doing this – he chose to obey God rather than man. Sometimes obedience to God is costly and uncomfortable, but even then it results in blessing. Bunyan's book has, over the intervening centuries, strengthened and encouraged huge numbers of people globally. The story of *The Pilgrim's Progress* has helped its readers to understand how God works in the lives of each individual who chooses to follow him.

Question 39 – Do Christians have to obey the Church?

Church?

Where humans are involved, imperfection follows. As the church by definition involves human beings, the question of obedience to the church is particularly important; this may present a real difficulty for some people. Some of us are more sceptical than others, but we all appreciate that even good people are not always everything they should be. We may also have differing ideas of what is meant by 'the church'. In some people's perception this is a huge institution; maybe the Roman Catholic Church or the Church of England (Anglican), and there may be particular concerns associated with this understanding. Other people may just think of the local church of whatever hue and have concerns about the local leadership. And so, whatever comes to mind when thinking about 'the church' there may be real concerns. This brings us to the question of whether or not Christians have to obey the church.

Joining Commitments

No matter what type of organisation we think about, membership normally entails complying with some rules. Often this includes a rule that members must not bring the organisation into disrepute. In the case of a church, there will be something that is usually referred to as a 'statement of faith' which defines the core teachings that the church subscribes to, and which anyone wanting to become a member must accept. There may also be unwritten rules about how members conduct themselves in church services or meetings, and also expectations of how people conduct themselves generally. For instance, a church might well exclude someone who insists on living in an immoral way. Most people will accept such 'rules' as being perfectly reasonable, even if they wish that some of them were different.

Surely Not

It is probable that, for most of us, the first thing that comes into our minds when we think about 'obeying the church' is something other than what we have looked at so far. We are likely to be thinking in terms of whether we are expected to 'do what you are told'; whether or not we are required to submit to other people. Whatever stance a particular local church might take on this, the fact is that the New Testament writers are quite clear that there is a responsibility upon Christians to be submitted: first of all to God, then to leaders within the church, and then to one another. Before throwing our hands up in horror, let's look at the reason for this, and what being submitted actually means in practice.

Please bear in mind that we are discussing whether Christians need to submit – this certainly doesn't apply to anyone who is not yet a Christian. Under the previous question we considered whether Christians have to obey God; clearly submission to God must precede submission to the local church. It doesn't make sense for someone who is a Christian to not be submitted to God, but it is certain that if they are not submitted to God then they will never submit to human authority. And so, in answering the current question we will assume acceptance of the need to be submitted to God, as explained under the previous topic.

Accountability

We need to look at why the New Testament writers tell Christians to submit to church leaders. This is explained by the writer of the book that is addressed to the Hebrews, who states:

> Have confidence in your leaders and submit to their authority, because they keep watch over you as those who must give an account. Do this so that their work will be a joy, not a burden, for that would be of no benefit to you.[1]

This passage is noteworthy in that it points out that those who have leadership responsibility and authority are also accountable to God for the way that they fulfil that responsibility and exercise that authority. This is similar to a passage in the New Testament letter of James, which states that those who teach will be held accountable for their teaching.[2] God gives authority to leaders, but he also holds them accountable, which is reassuring to know.

Alarm Bells

The apostle Paul, in his letter to the church in Ephesus, instructs them (us) to "submit to one another." [3] This is clearly going beyond just those in leadership in the church, and to us today may sound quite alarming. We need to appreciate that the context here is rather different to what we might be imagining. For someone whose concept of church involves a sharp differentiation between those who are 'ministers' (clergy) and those who form the church congregation, submission to other members of the church seems inappropriate.

A New Pattern

We need to recognise that this differentiation is not the pattern for church that we see in the New Testament writings, and neither is it the pattern followed by many churches today. The idea of a separation between those seen as 'ministers' from the church as a whole is rooted in the Old Testament; this is at odds with the pattern for church that we read about in the New Testament books and letters.

The New Testament pattern for church is for one cohesive body, albeit with different members having differing God-given gifts, and different roles (both formal and informal) that reflect those gifts. After the time when the New Testament was written, the church gradually morphed, changing from the church pattern that we can see evidenced within the New Testament writings. This resulted in a strongly hierarchical structure that recognised particular ministry gifts, and either ignored others or downplayed them.

In reality every Christian should expect to be pulling their weight; exercising the gift(s) that God has given them. And so, it is not only those who are specifically recognised as leaders within the church who are able to minister to others. Every Christian can, and should, be ministering according to the way that God has chosen to work in and through them.[4] When the church comes together, all can have something to contribute, both to the church as a whole, and to individuals. [5]

So, what does submission to one another amount to? It comes down to recognising the gifts of God in other people, allowing each other the freedom to function within their gift(s), and receiving the benefits that come from this exercise of God-given gifting. Where churches behave in this way everyone benefits; each person is able to give to others, and everyone receives from God through the ministry of one another.

Question 40 – What does the Bible mean by 'Grace'?

Out on a Limb

One Thursday in the summer of 1973 I had the job of painting a bare brick wall. It was inevitably a dull task, involving a whole day working the bristles of the brush into every crevice and imperfection in the mortar, aiming for the outcome of a perfectly white wall. Tedious though the job was, this was actually helpful to me because it gave me the opportunity to think. On that particular day I had a great deal to think about.

Some ten days previously I had written to a young lady to tell her that I had been praying about who I should marry and, specifically, that I had for some time been asking God about her. I explained that God had been encouraging me in this, and that I now felt it was time to speak to her. Jean had replied to my letter asking if we could meet up when she came to London the next week. On the Wednesday I took the train into the city, and then the Underground to North Finchley. It was with increasing nervousness that I walked to the street and to the house where Jean was staying. She answered my knock and led me to a small sitting room at the back of the house, where she offered me a cup of tea. Then Jean asked me to explain my letter. I basically repeated what I had written, adding only a few extra details. Jean seemed reasonably satisfied, and I waited to hear what she would say. Would she chastise me for my presumption? This was a huge step for me and, whilst I was trusting God that it was the right step, this didn't stop me from being very nervous – the truth is that Jean and I hardly knew each other.

Conversations with God

What transpired then was astonishing. Jean told me about some conversations that she had had with God two years previously, and how she had asked whether or not she was to be married. When God showed her that she would be, she set about praying for her future husband, asking for certain characteristics that she recognised would be important for her, and also asking for certain things to happen. Most of the Christian men that Jean knew were shorter than her; one thing that she had asked God for was that her husband would be taller. When I heard this my level of hope and confidence rose – I definitely fit the bill in that respect. She then explained how she had asked that if this man was not yet a Christian that he would become one, and that God would also bring him to study at the same Bible college as her. But the staggering thing was what Jean said next.

Instant Recognition

Jean explained that when the student body had come together for the first meeting of the next academic year, she looked across the room, saw me, and immediately knew in her spirit that I was the man that God had chosen for her, the man she would marry. We later compared notes and worked out that the very week that Jean was asking God about marriage, I was attending an annual Christian Convention in the English Lake District town of Keswick. Here I had learned about 'our' Bible College and had subsequently applied to study there. That evening when I left to travel home again, I was a different man. I now had an 'understanding' with this wonderful woman – surely we were to be married. I now had a massive amount to think through and process mentally but especially emotionally.

Why God?

The next day, while painting the wall, I was thinking intensely about what had transpired the previous afternoon. I was thrilled at what God had brought about, but at the same time really struggled to understand why God had done such a huge thing for me, and in such a marvellous way. I was quite certain that there was nothing that I had done to deserve this, and I felt as if my brain would explode as I sought to figure out the basis for what God had done for me. And then, eventually, it somehow dawned on me. God had brought this about because of one thing alone – because he loved me. It wasn't because of anything that I had done, it wasn't what I deserved; this was his unmerited favour, his grace shown towards me.

Christians understand the term grace, as used in the Bible, to mean God's undeserved love that he shows towards individuals. Grace tends to be thought of in the context of forgiveness, rather than in circumstances such as in the story above. But God doesn't see a divide between the 'spiritual' and the 'natural'. He loves people and delights in demonstrating his love for us in all sorts of ways.

Amazing Grace

Many people are familiar with the song "Amazing Grace" written by John Newton and first published in 1779. He had been an Atlantic slave trader until he cast himself upon God's mercy during a ship wreck experience in 1748; he subsequently became a Christian. The words of Amazing Grace encapsulate John Newton's story, and how God rescued him – not only physically but from himself as well.

The first verse reads:

> *Amazing grace! How sweet the sound*
>
> *That saved a wretch like me;*
>
> *I once was lost, but now am found;*
>
> *Was blind, but now I see.*

John Newton knew what his life had been like: displeasing to God; undeserving of God's favour. And yet he recognised God's hand in intervening in his life and bringing him to realise what Jesus had done, even for him, when Jesus gave his life, dying on a Roman cross.

This is the grace of God. He provided the way for us to be rescued from ourselves, from the consequences of our wrongdoing, guilt and shame. But not only did he provide a way for us to be set free, he also then sought us out and showed us his love. Grace is God's unmerited favour, his undeserved kindness. Grace is the opposite of the law that we see in the Old Testament; law binds us, but grace sets us free.

Misunderstanding

The apostle Paul writes about grace quite specifically in his New Testament letter to the Romans, seeking to guide the church's understanding. Certain Christians were going astray, using God's grace as an excuse to continue behaving wrongly. They thought that by continuing to live in a way that displeased God they were giving him an opportunity to show even more grace through forgiving them. Paul emphasises that this is totally false reasoning.[1] God's grace in forgiveness is there to set people free from their past, so that they can move forward into everything that he wants for them.[2] Although forgiveness is certainly available to cover whatever wrong Christians may continue to do, God calls them to live a new, transformed life where they seek to honour and serve him.[3]

This case recorded in Romans illustrates how some people latch onto particular Bible verses and, taking them out of context, use them to mean what they would like them to mean. But here Paul's comments about grace highlight the importance of context when understanding what the Bible has to tell us. The grace of God is hugely important; it is only because of his grace towards us that we have the opportunity to be reconciled to him. But God's grace goes beyond forgiveness; he also shows Christians how to live a truly good and fulfilling life and equips them to do just that.[4]

The Dining Room

❖ Question 41 – What is the church – an organisation?

Confusion Reigns

The term 'church' is used today to mean a variety of things, some of which are very different from the original use of the word. Everyone has their own idea of what is meant by the term. Many people use it to refer to an edifice on a street corner – a building. Some use 'church' to refer to an institution or organisation. Dictionaries list many different meanings. The problem is that the use of the word has morphed in multiple directions. To understand what the term 'church' is really meant to represent, we need to revert to how it was originally understood, as used in the text of the Bible.[1]

Origins

The New Testament was written in Greek; 'church' is the English word that is used to translate the Greek word 'ecclesia', from which we get the modern English term 'ecclesiastical' – meaning 'related to the church'. Although 'church' (ecclesia) is essentially linked to Christianity and occurs 114 times in the New Testament, it actually predates the Christian era. We find 'ecclesia' used more than a century before in the Greek translation of the books of the Old Testament. Essentially 'church' (or ecclesia) means an assembly of people.[2] It is important that we retain this basis for understanding what the church is – that church means people, not a physical structure nor an organisational entity. Any other use of 'church' is not something that is based upon the Bible.

The Christians in the time that the New Testament books were being written didn't have religious buildings to meet in; they met in people's homes.[3] This is not to suggest that local groups of Christians should not have a dedicated building to meet in today – we can all understand the practical benefit of this. Just as there were no church buildings, neither was there a church organisation. However, we can appreciate the benefit from having some degree of structure within the local church. This said, it is regrettable if common usage of the term effectively downgrades our

139

understanding of 'church' by using the term to mean either a physical building or an organisation.

A Different Understanding

Having returned to how the term 'church' was used in the Bible – to represent an assembly of God's people – what does this actually mean in practical terms? To appreciate this, we need first to understand that the church is a spiritual entity; in its very essence it is 'of God'. We need to look beyond our earthly understanding of things, recognising that the church refers to a group of people who have been set aside by God. The church consists of people who have each acknowledged God for who he is, have received God's forgiveness and cleansing for their wrongdoing, and who have dedicated their lives to live in a way that pleases him.[4] But there is more; the church is a collection of people who have the presence of God within them and who represent God in, and to, the world around. Buildings and organisations are insignificant when compared with this understanding of 'church'.

The Church Organism

Someone might suggest that there must surely be more to church than a loose collection of people, and they would of course be right; there is more. There is a structure to this body. In fact, the New Testament writers liken the church to a human body, with eyes, ears, limbs, etc.[5] The structure of the church is not supposed to be like a man-made organisation, but like an organism – an organism (body) which is made up of different parts that have different roles and abilities that have been given and assigned by God.[6] The cohesiveness of the church is achieved because every member is submitted to God, and every member is submitted to each other, recognising and releasing each other to function together as God has gifted each one. This is how the church is supposed to be, and what we should hope for it to be. In reality, however, the church is made up of people who still have flaws, and so it doesn't always represent God as well as it should. Sadly, these human weaknesses can result in a focus on the wrong things, such that the spiritual becomes sidelined. The Christian landscape is littered with religious 'debris' in the form of hierarchy and organisation where the spiritual plays little, if any part.

Lost the Plot

If the church were supposed to be an organisation, then it is patently a disorganised and fragmented one. Since the early centuries following the time of Jesus, the Christian church has experienced disunity with two major streams taking different routes: Eastern Orthodox and Roman Catholic. Since then the protestant reformation that began in 16th century Europe has spawned many other church denominations or organisations. Some people bemoan this disunity. And in one sense it is regrettable, but on the other hand, new things came into being which were prompted because of the unsatisfactory state of the old. The Christian church is not an organisation in the typical sense of the word. When that is what it becomes then that may be an indication that it has lost the plot, that it is failing to fulfil God's purpose.

Question 42 – Can I be a Christian and not go to church?

Why Wouldn't You?

The simple answer to this question is 'Yes'; becoming a Christian is about entering into a relationship with God. This does not necessarily involve the church. There are lots of people who identify as Christians who are not active members of a local church, but it would be completely wrong to leave the matter here. The real question is: 'Why would someone who has found forgiveness from God, and has committed their life to following Jesus, not want to be part of a local church?'

Potential Hindrances

There are various reasons why it might be difficult for someone to be involved with a local church. These may be physical: for instance, due to illness or serious disability; or through being posted abroad where there is no local church; or due to incarceration in prison. It might be that there is no genuine expression of church within a sensible travelling distance. However, these circumstances are exceptional. There are other, more personal reasons why some who have become Christians choose to shun church. Before we look at these let's first consider what reasons there are for being part of a church.

Togetherness

As we read the New Testament it is quite clear that every Christian needs to become part of their local Christian community. This is taught by the Bible writers, both implicitly and explicitly.[1] This is also the normal pattern that we see worked out in the New Testament narratives, specifically in the book known as the Acts of the Apostles, but also in the letters and books that follow.[2] And so from the perspective of the Bible, being part of the local church is the norm. In addition to this being the normal pattern, a Christian needs to be part of the local church because it is through the church that they will receive support and encouragement.[3] There is yet a third reason to be part of a local church; the church provides an environment where Christians can discover their God-given gifts and abilities, and can learn how to use these for the benefit of other people.

Nonsense

Some people are reluctant to join a local church because they want to 'do their own thing'; they don't like the idea of being a part of something where they need to accept what other people say. This sounds perfectly reasonable to us in the 21st century; we are used to 'paddling our own canoe', and we resist the idea of submitting ourselves to other people in any way. And yet it is important to realise that being submitted is a central part of what it means to be a Christian. First and foremost, a Christian needs to be submitted to God. It makes no sense for someone to claim to be a follower of Jesus, and then refuse to follow him, or refuse to submit their lives to his direction and guidance – to do so is a contradiction.[4] People who opt out of church often claim that they follow Jesus, but at the same time won't accept the authority of other Christians, that is to say the local church. However, this is also nonsense because the writers of the New Testament books make clear the importance of being in fellowship with other Christians. These first teachers of the Christian faith tell us that being submitted to one another is fundamental, not an optional extra. The apostle John tells us:

> For whoever does not love their brother and sister, whom they have seen, cannot love God, whom they have not seen.[5]

The same principle applies to being submitted; how can we claim to be submitted to God but then refuse to learn from other Christians, particularly from those in the church who God has assigned the responsibility to lead?[6]

Practical Application

It would be helpful here for us to consider what being part of a local church actually means. The first thing to note is that the church is not a religious club or society. If you have read the previous topic you will have seen how the writers of the New Testament liken the church to a human body, with different 'members' fulfilling different roles. When we speak of membership in the context of the local church we are not referring to 'being enrolled', but rather being committed to playing our respective parts in the body, and at the same time being committed to work in harmony with the other parts of the body. The local church provides the environment where we can explore our own areas of gifting and can benefit from the gifting that God has given to others. For instance, God places within the church those who have the spiritual gifting to teach. This is very important because people with this gift are equipped to explain what the Bible has to say and relate it to what people experience in their daily lives – something that benefits everyone, whether a new Christian or someone who has spent their lifetime following Jesus.

Damage Limitation

Some people are reluctant to join a local church because they have in the past experienced being hurt by 'church', or by individual Christians. This is an understandable reaction. Sadly, some people do cause hurt because we are all a 'work in progress', and we don't always behave in the way that God wants us to. There is absolutely no excuse for hurting one another; but neither is it right for us to be affronted when others act insensitively towards us. If we choose to find fault in one another then there will surely be plenty of opportunity to do so, but this is not how God wants us to behave. We find in the Gospel according to Matthew a conversation between the apostle Peter and Jesus:

> Then Peter came to Jesus and asked, "Lord, how many times shall I forgive my brother or sister who sins against me? Up to seven times?"
> Jesus answered, "I tell you, not seven times, but seventy times seven." [7]

Forgiveness is fundamental to being a Christian; it is only through being forgiven by God that anyone can become a Christian. But we are also instructed to forgive others – something that is included in the well-known Lord's Prayer that Jesus gave as an example to his disciples when they asked him how they should pray.[8]

Look Elsewhere

Maybe we should also consider one further reason that might make someone reluctant to be part of a local church: fear. For anyone who has no previous experience of church it could be quite daunting to turn up at an unfamiliar building, to meet with strangers, and to take part in something that is likely to be a totally new experience. In reality, churches that are based on the pattern taught in the New Testament are usually very welcoming and helpful to new people, and especially to anyone who has recently become a Christian. At the end of the day if you visit a church, but are not made to feel welcome, then you may be better to look elsewhere rather than returning to that particular church!

Question 43 – Do I have to give money if I go to church?

Get out of Jail Free

Money is a difficult issue for us all; usually what we have available is quite limited, and we know that we can only spend it, or give it, once. Unfortunately, the Christian church has a chequered history when it comes to seeking monetary support. The protestant reformation started in the year 1517 when a German monk, Martin Luther, nailed his '95 Thesis' to the door of Wittenburg Cathedral. This thesis was in part a protest against a despicable money-making scheme that was being perpetrated by the Roman Catholic Church, referred to as the 'doctrine of indulgences'. Without going into great detail, it is sufficient to explain that this scheme involved requiring donations of significant sums of money. In exchange for these 'gifts' the church would issue a certificate, rather like a 'get out of jail free card', that supposedly reduced the time that the person would need to spend in torment in purgatory after they died. Purgatory is a specific Roman Catholic teaching that is not considered in this book.

TV Today

In the modern era we may hear of some television evangelists, and personality orientated organisations, placing an inappropriate emphasis on requesting financial contributions. Many people are offended by such explicit schemes and can recognise that whatever the financial need that they are seeking to meet, the tactic for achieving this is not honouring to God. These schemes can seem greedy, but more to the point they are based on a wrong understanding of how God wants Christians to conduct ourselves.[1]

Being Realistic

We have to acknowledge that money is a sensitive area for those who give, or are asked to give, but that it is also a vital necessity for enabling any organisation to function. Churches need money to pay staff, maintain facilities and support community and mission work. Also, churches often have funds that are specifically allocated to meet urgent pastoral needs within the community. What we can all understand is that money is most certainly needed.

The simple answer to the question about giving money to church is that no, of course you don't have to give, and certainly not if you are a visitor or guest. The financial support of the local church is the responsibility of those who are committed members of that church. That said, visitors may well take account of why they have attended the church meeting, and whether they feel that they would like to make a financial contribution. After all, we don't usually expect to attend other events without it costing us something.

Intimidation

Just as there are obvious excesses related to asking for money, there can also be implicit pressures related to financial giving. Some churches have a time in services when people are invited to give; perhaps a collection plate or bag is passed around. This practice might be difficult for someone who is not able to give or didn't wish to. It would be regrettable for anyone to feel intimidated by this practice such that they avoid visiting a Christian church because of it.

Shoe String Budgeting

There is a related issue; the 'collection plate' can lead to the idea that all that is necessary is to give small change, or maybe to stretch this to a bank note or two.[2] This approach to giving is unrealistic in terms of the finances of any church; the needs are far greater than can be met by everyone donating small change. For some, this small change mentality has extended into the idea that everything associated with the Christian church should be done on a shoe-string budget. They expect that churches and Christian-based organisations should be tight for funds, employ poorly paid staff, etc. Where this is the perception, then those churches and Christian organisations that are properly funded may be seen as tainted, suspected of wrongdoing, or at least of asking for more than is 'appropriate' from members or supporters.

Being Serious

In reality, where churches are well funded this is more likely to be because church members take the matter of giving seriously.[3] This happens where

Christians recognise the need to properly resource the church, and where their commitment to serve God is translated into practical action – right the way through to financial giving. The Christian perspective on giving is less to do with need and much more about honouring God. Those who are trusting God for their wellbeing, and who recognise his hand of blessing upon their lives, often give of their resources in response to him. This is actually a biblical principle that is enshrined in the Old Testament pattern of giving a percentage of income.

Question 44 – Does it matter which church I belong to?

Why do it?

Attending a church does not have any value in itself. It is not something that we should ever do for the sake of it. The value of a church 'service' is that it is an opportunity to join together with other people to worship God; that is to recognise God for who he is and to express this.[1] That is the essence of worship.

In a church service this expression is likely to include singing songs that praise God for his attributes, and that remind everyone of his love and purposes for them. It will probably involve short sections of the Bible being read, and also some form of helpful and encouraging talk about God and what the Bible has to say in relation to people's lives. This talk is often referred to as 'preaching' or a 'sermon'. Joining with other people is in itself an important part of a church service, giving opportunity to chat together and to encourage one another.[2]

Imitations

When we consider the question 'which church?' the important thing is that the church should be focussed on what God intends church to be. This can't be taken for granted with everything that calls itself 'church'. In the Study Room we looked at what is meant by 'orthodox' Christian belief; there are groups of people who claim to be Christian but who deviate from orthodox belief. This means that they are missing the foundations upon which genuine Christian faith is based; their belief systems are imitations and not truly Christian at all.

There are groups such as Mormons, Jehovah's Witnesses, 'Christian Scientists' and Unitarians, amongst others, which do not adhere to orthodox Christian theology.[3] Such groups should definitely be avoided because they do not hold to the truth about God, and are misleading and unhelpful for anyone who genuinely wants a relationship with God.[4]

Differentiators

Those churches that hold to an orthodox understanding of who God is cover a diverse range of styles, religious practices, and beliefs about specific aspects of Christianity. Of these, one of the main differentiators is between those that have a strong 'religious' focus, based on traditions that have built up over a long period of time, and those that are focussed on following closely to what the New Testament writers tell us about the Christian life, and about what it means to be a Christian community. It may be helpful to refer back to the topic in the Lounge section: 'If I became a Christian would I have to become "religious?"' (Q 23).

The easiest way to know where a church stands is to ask if the church is 'evangelical' in its teaching. If it is, then it should be focussed on teaching what the New Testament has to say – this is important. Some churches actually have the name 'Evangelical Church', but most churches that are evangelical in their teaching don't actually reflect this in their name. If you accept and take to heart what you read in this book, then it is important to find a church that is firmly based on what the New Testament has to say to us. This isn't just a matter of what a particular church teaches, but also what it does – how it reflects God's love to people outside of the church.

Decision Making

For all that we might say about the pros and cons of particular types of church, this is only 'information'. If you decide in future to become a Christian, or if you already are, then the important thing is to ask God to guide you in your decision about a church. Ask him to show you which church he wants you to be a part of. Ask God to lead you to the place that will be a blessing to you, where you will be able to grow in your life as a Christian. If you ask, then be sure to follow the guidance that God gives.[5] Don't allow yourself to be distracted into settling for somewhere different. See the last topic within the 'The Contract' section of this book (Q 70).

Question 45 – Is it better to belong to a traditional church?

New Kids on the Block

Over recent decades, in the UK and elsewhere, there has been an upsurge in new style churches. These 'new kids on the block' are thriving and growing apace. In fact, these groups typically have within their DNA a focus on 'planting' more churches in other cities, towns and villages, so as to reach people there with the Christian message of hope and new life.[1] These churches are usually characterised by high commitment and energy, and close adherence to the pattern for church that can be seen within the pages of the New Testament.

At first glance this sounds very attractive for anyone who becomes a Christian and who wants to take their faith seriously – and quite rightly so. To be balanced, however, we must recognise that just as 'traditional' is not necessarily a bad thing, so also 'new' is not necessarily a good thing.

As a generalisation one could suggest that the traditional denominations are encumbered with structure and practices that impede them from being everything that the New Testament suggests that church should be. Equally we could suggest that because the new style churches are less structured, there is greater freedom to become unbalanced. Both of these suggestions are undoubtedly true. And so we come back to the question for this topic – which is best?

The answer has to be that each type should be taken on merit. That might seem obvious, but for many people there are other factors that come into play.

Bad Reasons for a Bad Choice

There are reasons why someone might think that it is better to belong to a traditional church, not least of which is confidence. Many people are risk-averse and will generally tend to choose the 'known path' rather than trying something new. This might entail returning to the traditional type of church that they maybe went to when younger. It might simply amount to being conventional. Someone might feel sorry for a traditional church that is struggling for numbers, and feel that it would be good to 'support' this rather than opting to join one of the new type of churches. There could be a good reason for choosing a traditional 'denominational' church, but it won't be one of those suggested here – they are all bad reasons for potentially making a bad choice. Bad, because they are based upon caution or sentiment, rather than upon sound and positive reasoning.

Some people are inherently inclined towards the 'new', which may give them a propensity to feel drawn towards one of the new style churches. They may be attracted to what is typically the younger demographic of a new style church, or because the worship music is more to their taste, the preaching more dynamic, or the projected graphics more contemporary. These again are all bad reasons for potentially making a bad choice. Bad because they are based on prejudice or external factors, rather than what is really important.

Good Reasons for a Good Choice

And so, having outlined those things that are not a valid basis for choosing a church, we need to think about what a sound basis would be for making a decision.

Whatever 'considerations' are taken account of, when it comes to choosing which church to join there is no substitute for asking God for guidance. Sadly, for many this isn't the first step – but maybe it should be! For a Christian who is intent upon honouring God, the selection of a church is a very important decision, and so asking God makes perfect sense – and he will certainly want to steer them in this.[2] That said, there are some considerations that need to be borne in mind, for which I refer you to the previous topic.

Of Real Importance

Overall, the question isn't about whether to be part of a traditional or a new style church. The important thing is to be in the place where you will be blessed and in the context where you will best be able to serve God. This comes down to what the church teaches and how closely it matches the pattern that is exemplified in the pages of the New Testament. Being part of a church isn't only about receiving; it is also about being encouraged, equipped and released to serve others, whether in the local church or community, or beyond.[3]

Question 46 – What does it mean to be a Pentecostal Christian?

Another Differentiator

In the previous questions in the Dining Room we have considered different types of church and highlighted the benefit of joining a church that is evangelical in its teaching. This means a church where the basis of belief and practice is the New Testament rather than religious traditions that have crept in over time. Now, under the current question, we need to consider another differentiator between churches, which comes down to how a church views the Holy Spirit.

The Gift

The Holy Spirit tends to be referred to as the 'third person' of the Trinity (see the Study Room – Q 9). It is essential to understand that the Holy Spirit is indeed a person – referred to as 'he' and definitely not as 'it'.[1] Within the New Testament is the book of the Acts of the Apostles. It tells the story of the early Christians, starting from the point when Jesus, having risen from the dead, was about to ascend into heaven. The story begins by telling us what Jesus said to his followers immediately before his ascension: that they were to receive a gift from God, namely, the coming of the Holy Spirit. Jesus told his followers:

> *"Do not leave Jerusalem, but wait for the gift my Father promised, which you have heard me speak about. For John baptised with water, but in a few days you will be baptised with the Holy Spirit."*[2]

The Power of God

Jesus' followers obeyed his instructions and waited, and days later they experienced the coming of the Holy Spirit in a dramatic way.[3] This happened at the time that the Jewish people were celebrating their feast of Pentecost, which is where the term 'Pentecostal' comes from. 'Pentecostal' is used to refer to the experience of those initial believers. Today we refer to someone as Pentecostal if they have experienced the Holy Spirit's anointing upon their lives and are serving God with the power that the Holy Spirit provides.

'Pentecostal' is a term that is associated with some churches, i.e. they are 'Pentecostal churches'. More commonly Christians use a different term to describe the same thing: the word 'charismatic'. This term derives from the Greek word used in the original language of the New Testament – 'charis', meaning 'gift'. A charismatic Christian is someone who believes in and has received one or more of the gifts that God the Holy Spirit gives to individuals as promised in the Bible verses quoted above. [4] Many churches will describe themselves as charismatic, although rarely is this term used in the name of a local church.

Strange Ideas

There are churches that are evangelical but do not believe that the Holy Spirit still gives spiritual gifts to Christians today. They teach that the gifts are something that Christians experienced during New Testament times, but that they have since disappeared from the church and are no longer available for Christians to receive. This idea is at odds with the actual experience of millions of Christians today who have direct experience of the gifts and empowering of the Holy Spirit. But then if everything that calls itself 'church' was the same, we wouldn't be considering some of the questions in this section.

The Bathroom

❖ Question 47 – What do Christians mean by the term 'sin'?

Terminology

We all identify with the words 'guilt', 'shame' and 'conscience'; these are things that we feel within ourselves. 'Sin' is different. Sin relates to something that we do that is directed against God. In essence, the root of all sin is opposition to God.

Someone who believes that there is no God will not have a sense of sin. This does not mean that they do not sin, but simply that they are unable to recognise sin in themselves. This is why throughout this book the use of the term 'sin' has been largely avoided, the words guilt, shame and conscience being used in preference.

Not Optional

However, sin is a very important concept. We all sin, whether we choose to acknowledge God or not.[1] For someone considering the claims of Christianity, sin needs to be understood and faced up to. Receiving forgiveness for our sin against God is fundamental to becoming a Christian – God has provided a way for our sin to be forgiven, for it to be removed from us completely.[2] It is only as a result of this that we can then have a relationship with God.

Missing the Target

Some people have linked the term 'sin' with the ancient art of archery; sin is like an arrow that is shot from a bow and fails to reach the target, falling short. In archery this would have been very significant because an arrow failing to reach its target would have had serious consequences – life-threatening consequences. If the archer's quarry was an animal then it would have had the chance to escape, and there may not have been food on the table. Even worse, if the quarry was a human adversary; failure to stop him could well result in the archer's own death. Often Christians will use this concept from archery, referring to us 'falling short' of what God requires, failing to live rightly.

157

This idea of falling short is used in the New Testament by the apostle Paul, who writes "for all have sinned and fall short of the glory of God."[3] Paul doesn't say this to condemn, but is simply stating a fact – we have all fallen short in the way we have lived; none of us is good enough to be accepted by God. However, this isn't the end of what Paul has to say on the matter. Paul goes on to put this in context by explaining how, in spite of our sinful condition, God has made a way for us to be restored to himself. This is through what Jesus achieved when he surrendered his life in our stead, thereby taking the consequences of our sin upon himself.

Called to be...

Having outlined what the term 'sin' means, it would be helpful now to think about what constitutes sin. This comes down to anything that displeases God. God created us to fulfil his high calling upon our lives. He made us to live in relationship with himself and, effectively, to be his agents on earth and to act on his behalf. We see this outlined in the first chapter of the Bible, right at the beginning in the book of Genesis. Here God's words are recorded:

> God blessed them and said to them, "Be fruitful and increase in number; fill the earth and subdue it. Rule over the fish in the sea and the birds in the sky and over every living creature that moves on the ground."[4]

Let's Compare – Not!

As human beings we have a tendency to operate on what might be called 'comparative morality'; we choose to determine how 'good' or 'bad' we are by evaluating ourselves against what we think other people are like. We do this in a similar way to how some people determine their own value by comparing their income with that of others, or by comparing their home or car, or the holidays that they take. God, however, uses absolute values – by these there is no one who comes up squeaky clean, in fact nowhere near.[5]

Deep Insight

There is nothing superficial about how God looks at us – no looking just at what is on the surface. This is highlighted by God's words, as recorded in one of the history books of the Old Testament: "People look at the outward appearance, but the Lord looks at the heart."[6] The idea that sin isn't just about our outward actions is also emphasised by the words of Jesus in the New Testament: "But I tell you that anyone who looks at a woman lustfully has already committed adultery with her in his heart."[7] When God judges us he sees everything; he knows exactly what we are like. Everything that God sees in us that he is not pleased to see, is sin.

Someone might ask "what does it matter"? There are two reasons why it does matter very much. Firstly, because it saddens God to see us living in ways that prevent us from fulfilling our full potential, being less than we could be. And secondly, because our sin has created a barrier between us and God – it separates us from God. We all understand how harmful broken relationships are; a broken relationship with God is the ultimate break and has the greatest possible consequence for us.

Big Mistake

Some people emphasise God's love, suggesting that everything will be all right in the end: "A loving God won't really reject us when it comes down to it." This idea is so very wrong; it is predicated upon a wrong understanding of who God is and a wrong understanding of who we are. God is so much more than we are, in every way. He is infinite and is morally pure. According to the Bible we are his creation, being formed in his image – meaning that there are things about us that are God-like. His calling upon us is based on who he has made us to be, which is far more than we usually choose to be or allow ourselves to become.

God lays out his calling and his purpose for us, but then we are given a choice. We can continue to muddle through life, falling short, or we can step up to the mark and choose to live his way. If we choose to live according to God's high calling, then he has provided a way for us to be 'made clean'. That is, to be forgiven for all the wrong we have done in the past, whether in thought, word or deed. If we choose to reject both God's high calling upon us, and his offer of forgiveness for our sin, then because God created us to be moral beings, the consequences of our decision are our own responsibility – they are ours alone. We are responsible for our lives now, and for our eternal destiny (see Q18).

Question 48 – What do I see when I look in the mirror?

Wishful Thinking

In the classical Grimm's fairy story of Snow White and the Seven Dwarfs, the evil queen looks into the magic mirror and utters the words, "Mirror, mirror, on the wall, who is the fairest one of all?" To her disgust, the mirror reveals the image of Snow White, rather than of herself. Magic mirrors are the stuff of fairy tales. When you or I look in the mirror we are unlikely to see the 'fairest one of all' reflected back to us. We see not an image of perfection, but rather a reflection of the stark reality of who we are, especially if we take a peek first thing in the morning.

A Cover Up

Most people value mirrors and use them often. This may be to assist us in personal grooming, or to check that garments are sitting correctly on our bodies; both aimed at ensuring that we look presentable. Some people don't like mirrors because they don't like themselves, while others may use a mirror to help them change their appearance. There is a 'deals' company that sends me emails each day with an eclectic mix of reduced price offers; I occasionally buy a restaurant voucher or something for the home. Recently there was an offer for a Make-Up Master Class – not something of any interest to me, except that I was struck by the model in the accompanying picture. Her makeup was being applied meticulously; it was a work of art. Her face was free from any blemish, her lips carefully outlined; but it was her eyes that were striking, they were dramatically enhanced. The image in the picture was probably digitally edited, but in any case it was unreal. This was an artificial portrayal of a person rather than the girl herself. A little makeup is one thing; this was theatrical in effect – rather like an actor playing someone totally different to who they actually are.

Public Image

What do we see when we look in the mirror? It is pretty certain that what we see is not perfection. There will be the usual blemishes of one sort or another, there may be frown lines or laugh lines, our complexion may not be pleasing to us. Whatever we see, for many of us our appearance will not be quite what we would wish it to be like. However we appear, this physical presentation is merely the external 'face', the public image. The more important thing that we see is reflected back to us when we look into our own eyes.

The Eyes Have it

According to an old proverb, the eyes are the 'windows of the soul.' When we look to see the 'real me', how do we feel about what we see then? Of course, the eyes are only an anatomical feature, a mechanism for seeing, and yet they are so important; they are the feature of our bodies that communicates more than all of the others taken together. We have the expression 'to catch someone's eye'; just an instant of focus that signals recognition, need, and feelings as well. The expressiveness and communication associated with eyes never fails to amaze me; somehow they really do function as windows into what is going on inside of us. And so, when I look at my reflection in the mirror and into my own eyes, my soul is bared – there is no place to hide. What I see is what I am.

Imprints

We carry within ourselves the hurts of the past, the guilt of wrong actions, the consequences of wrong decisions, and maybe a bruised conscience – shame. A stranger who looks into our eyes may see a hint of our emotional scars; but when we look at our own reflection we see more deeply because we know what lies beneath.

Slave or Free?

The Christian message is one of freedom.[1] This may seem strange to anyone who believes themselves to be at liberty already, but although most of us are free to walk around without external constraint, there are inner constraints that mean we are anything but free. We are slaves to our past and to our consciences, slaves to our sense of shame. The Christian message is that God knows what lies within us; he knows it even more clearly than we do ourselves. Because he knows this and because he cares deeply about us, he has provided a way for you and me to be set free.[2] This is exactly why Jesus gave his life for us: to make a way for God to forgive, to release us from the prison of our own guilt-ridden consciences and to make us completely 'clean' to his all-seeing eyes.[3] When we ask God to free us from our own past, he does so and also creates a way for us to be friends with himself – a way for us to start again. Then when we look into the reflection of our own eyes, what we will see looking back is completely different to before, something new – we will see promise, we will see hope.[4]

❖ Question 49 – Can I get free from shame and guilt?

Beneficial Pain

We are all aware of having a conscience, something within us that causes us discomfort whenever we behave badly. Admittedly some people's consciences are more finely tuned than others, and some have suppressed this sensitivity such that they barely notice it at all. However, if you are reading this book then you are likely to have a sense of 'right and wrong' and to be aware that your conscience is active and functioning. Some might wish that they didn't have this sensitivity, or that it wasn't so strong, but our conscience is part of how God has made us, and is something to be grateful for. As I write these words, we are experiencing a wet spring morning, dull and dreary, but I know that the rain is good, that my garden needs it, and that we will see the benefit of it in the days ahead. The pricking of our consciences can be similar – not enjoyable at the time but intended for our benefit.

Triggers

Our consciences tell us about our immediate decisions and actions and also about the things that we have done wrong in the past. It is as though we have a 'conscience history', an accumulation of guilt for all that we have done that we know to be wrong and that we are ashamed of. It is important to recognise that our consciences are influenced by our own personal moral codes; we may feel guilty about something that isn't actually wrong, or we may *not* be feeling guilty about something that *is* actually wrong. Some religious systems are 'heavy' on guilt, placing burdens upon people that God certainly doesn't intend for us. Most of the time however, our consciences trouble us because we are actually doing wrong – in thought, word or deed.

Feeling Bad

The message of the Bible is that we are all guilty of wrongdoing and should expect that our consciences will point this out.[1] The Bible tells us about how God wants us to behave, which in itself may reveal our guilt for not living in this way. But there is a third, and overarching, message of the Bible which is apparent from start to finish: we can be forgiven; we can be freed from a troubled conscience. Although the Bible writers do talk about conscience, the Bible is sharply focussed on the term 'sin'. Conscience is about how we feel and is based on what we believe to be right and wrong. Sin, on the other hand is based on what God holds as being right or wrong. We sin against God when we do what is wrong, based on his standards. Our consciences are a good indicator about right and wrong, but they aren't necessarily fully attuned to what God says.

Parallel Pathway

We have looked at several different terms – conscience, guilt, shame and sin. Our consciences are attuned to right and wrong, based partly on our own moral compass. When our consciences trouble us we feel a sense of guilt, and if we acknowledge this guilt we feel ashamed (shame). Sin is like a parallel pathway; sin is the wrong that we do based on what God says is wrong. When we know that we have sinned, then our consciences will trouble us, with the result that we will feel guilt and shame.[2] The forgiveness that God offers us is forgiveness for sin – the purpose of this forgiveness is that our guilt before God is taken away. When this happens our consciences are cleared, and we no longer have cause to feel ashamed.

Free Offer

The answer to the question about whether or not we can be free from shame and guilt is – yes, we can. This is because we can ask God to forgive us for everything that we have done wrong. This forgiveness is freely available to anyone, through what Jesus did for us when he died for mankind on the cross. Rather than explain here the details of how to receive this forgiveness, I refer you to the last section of this book – the 'The Contract' section.

Question 50 – How can God love me?

Reality

Do you come across as a confident, self-assured, positive person? If this is how others see you then what about how you actually feel on the inside? Are you carrying a heavy load: the burden of guilt, rejection, uncertainty or a general sense of feeling lost?

How we present ourselves outwardly is often at odds with how we feel about ourselves on the inside. Most of us project the pretence that our life is ok. We don't let people into our 'inner sanctum', the place where the real 'me' dwells, because we fear that they won't like what they see and may reject the person who we really are.

Honest to God

So, how about God – if we don't feel able to let other people know how we really feel about ourselves, and can't reveal to them what is going on deep inside, then what about God who knows the most intimate and deeply hidden details of our hearts?[1] Are we able to be honest to God? There is obviously a big difference in that we have to make a choice to reveal ourselves to another human being, whereas God already knows what we are like – totally. We might want to talk to him to explain how we really feel about ourselves, but actually he knows us inside out, from start to finish.[2] Given his understanding of who we are, can God love us the way that we are?

One might give a straightforward answer and say that, yes, of course he does, and that really would be true. But that is too simplistic – not because there are any caveats attached, but because knowing what we do about ourselves, we will probably struggle to believe this simple answer.

No Surprises

God knows that we are broken people. He is well aware of our individual histories and the things that have influenced us, moulded us and made us who we are. He is also aware of our inner desires and motives that result in the bad choices that we have made in the past. With God there are no delusions, no surprises. He simply wants to free us and give us the opportunity to make a fresh start. He offers to clear the slate and show us how to live rightly. God gives us the opportunity to make a new choice – a choice to align ourselves with himself, to commit to working out our lives so as to fulfil his purpose for us. But how can we know that this is true?

There are two things that point to this conclusion: the first is summarised in the person of Jesus Christ; the second is found in various places in the Bible where we can read of God's commitment to us and his understanding of what we are truly like.

Before looking at these two things that evidence God's love for us, we really should answer the actual question for this topic – how can God love me? The answer is that he is not like us. We cannot grasp how unlike us God is.[3] The Bible tells us that we were made in his image.[4] This is certainly true, but he is not a reflection of us – it is the other way around. We are a dim reflection of who God is. Dim because we have allowed ourselves to be tarnished, spoiled. We are like a mirror that hardly functions for the purpose for which it was originally made; the image has become pale and indistinct.

Almost Unthinkable

As human beings we struggle to love what is not like us, and so we wonder how God can love us when we have become so unlike him. The fact is that God loves us because he decided that he would – the Bible tells us that this was a decision that God made before he even created the world.[5] He loves us in spite of how we are and in spite of whom we have become. This is hard for us to understand, but we can accept that it is true. We can agree that the almost unthinkable is a fact, and we can respond to God.

The Plan

God's love for us, as we are, is evidenced in the person of Jesus. This may seem trite, but the facts speak for themselves. To start with, we are faced with the Bible's assertion that Jesus is the Son of God. This isn't some vague claim or some gloss on the evidence. Jesus' status is clear from the promises

166

and prophesies contained within the Old Testament writings, from his own assertion, from the testimony of God himself, and also from the teaching of the writers of the New Testament books. [6] The point is that God planned before the creation of the world that he would send his son, Jesus, to rescue mankind.[7] He planned this even before we became rebellious, before we started to sin, before we became what we are today. God understood how we would choose to be, and he put in place his rescue plan for the people that he knew we would become.

A Dire State

We can read of the dire things that God's people got up to at times during the period of the Old Testament. We read how those people slipped into abhorrent practices associated with worshipping 'other gods'. How individuals who were known for their faith in God still failed dramatically. And how as a nation God's people stopped worshipping him almost totally. And yet even after all of this, God sent his only son to suffer horribly so that he could rescue us. Does God care about our sin? Yes, of course he does – and he loves us in spite of it; in spite of our previous rejection of both himself and his purposes for us.

The Promise

There are numerous places in the Bible where we are shown that God knows what we are like, but that he still promises us a new life in spite of this:

> "Come now, let us settle the matter," says the Lord. "Though your sins are like scarlet, they shall be as white as snow; though they are red as crimson, they shall be like wool." [8]

> But he was pierced for our transgressions, he was crushed for our iniquities; the punishment that brought us peace was on him, and by his wounds we are healed.[9]

How can God love me? Quite simply because he has chosen to.[10]

Question 51 – Why am I the way I am?

Ancestors

'Who do you think you are?' is the name of a long-running TV series in the UK. Each programme follows a different well-known personality as they undertake research into their ancestry. Starting with parents and grandparents, they peel back the generations, looking closely at particular individuals along the way. Invariably this is an emotional experience as each participant learns new things about their forebears – sometimes praiseworthy, sometimes the opposite. They may learn about hardships that an ancestor faced; perhaps due to misfortune, or occasionally because of bad character or at least bad choices.

Whilst any one of us may choose to research our own individual ancestry, we can also look at the much bigger picture of who we are – our deepest roots and the things that have contributed to how we have developed. In the early chapters of the first book of the Bible we are told how everything began, starting with the first man and woman, Adam and Eve. We are not told very much about them initially, other than that God created them, placed them in the Garden of Eden, gave them things to do, and then stipulated just one simple rule that they must follow.[1] So far so good.

Big Deal

Where the story gets interesting is when it is suggested to these two people that they disobey God, that they ignore the one rule that he gave them to follow. The Bible gives us to understand that this was the first example of temptation that mankind ever encountered. It was a test that our original forebears failed dramatically.

In modern mythology this is all about an apple, which surely shouldn't be a big deal. But actually it was a monumentally big deal. Not because this pair chose to eat an apple (or whatever fruit it actually was), but because they chose, quite deliberately, to set themselves in opposition to what God had explicitly told them. They chose to defy God, to rebel.

A Quaint Tale

The tempter had told them two things: firstly, that the fruit would be rather good to eat; and secondly that the consequences would be positive rather than negative.[2] They fell for this story hook, line and sinker. You could consider this to be simply a quaint tale about someone else's mistake. But the message of this story in the book of Genesis, right at the beginning of the Bible, is that this one act of defiance set mankind on a course that has resulted in our being as we are today. The story of this event from our earliest history is hugely relevant to you and to me. From the time of Adam and Eve the human race has been in rebellion against our creator, against God.

This one act of rebellion is referred to technically as 'original sin' – it was the original sinful act that caused the rift between us and God. You and I are tainted by it, and from birth we each suffer the consequences of it.

Objection!

Before anyone raises an objection to this idea, suggesting that this can't possibly be fair, let's just take a reality check. If Adam and Eve, who experienced a close relationship with God, rebelled against him, how many of us would really have acted differently?[3] How many of us, given a fresh start would not at some point do just what we wanted, rather than obey God? It is a consequence of the free will that God has given us that we are able to choose for ourselves what we will do; we have freedom to defy God if we so choose.

The consequence of Adam and Eve's wrong choice is that we now live in separation from God. There is a gulf between us and God, a distance that we are unable to bridge. This change in mankind has meant that we have become inherently self-orientated, self-centred.

My Decision

We are apt to make choices based on what we think will be in the best interests of 'me'. We are selfish. Of course, this isn't always the case; we are not totally spoiled. We are capable of sacrificial acts, of generosity, of showing kindness when we don't have to. But our behaviour is based on the code of conduct that we have created for ourselves; we decide for ourselves what is right and what is wrong. We don't see why we should do what someone else tells us, not even when that someone else is God.

The Dynamics

We can all appreciate that the way we are reflects how we feel inside. We may feel hurt about the things that have been done to us in the past, resentful of the opportunities denied to us, envious of those who can enjoy things that we cannot. We may be hampered by our own sense of failure. We may be proud and boastful of our own sense of success. There are so many dynamics at work in us that make us the way that we are, but they all stem from that single act of our original forebears. Everyone is flawed.[4] Other people's flaws impact us, and ours impact other people as well as ourselves.

Let's Go Back

The question was posed in an earlier paragraph: 'How many of us, given a fresh start would not at some point do just what we wanted, rather than obey God?' It is clear from what the writers of the New Testament tell us that we do actually have this opportunity to have a fresh start – that is, for the slate to be wiped clean. When Jesus died on the cross he recovered what had been lost for us by the first man, Adam – Jesus is sometimes referred to as the 'second Adam'. The result of Adam's choice to defy God was condemnation for all of his descendants. The result of Jesus' obedience, even to suffering a horrible death, brings the opportunity for forgiveness and reconciliation to anyone who will ask to receive this.[5] So we can, in effect, go back. We can be made completely clean and start afresh with a new direction and purpose.

Question 52 – How can I believe in God when Christians have caused me hurt?

Ambassadors

This is a very difficult topic; not because it is difficult to answer, but because it reflects the very real hurt that we can each experience. Sadly, some people who claim to be Christians (and maybe actually are) can be the cause of deep grief to others who do not yet have a relationship with God – and for that matter also to those who do. The role of each true Christian is to be an ambassador for God.[1] It is therefore perfectly reasonable for other people to expect them to behave as such. For the person who is a Christian, all of their words and actions reflect upon God whom they proclaim and whom they seek to represent.

It's a Process

It must be understood that when someone becomes a Christian this doesn't make them perfect. It does free them from the guilt associated with their past life and does set them on a new trajectory for their future, but the impact of these changes needs to be worked out in practice. One would certainly hope, and expect, that the change in the life of the new Christian will be noticeable, but it will inevitably amount to only the initial steps in a good direction. There is a saying that 'Rome was not built in a day'. The same applies to the man or woman of God; they are each a work in progress.

Is it Surprising?

Imperfect people cause problems for other imperfect people. This is not for one moment to make excuses, but purely to highlight the point. None of us will reach perfection this side of the grave. There are references to 'genuine Christians' in various places in this book, meaning to infer that some who claim that they are Christian are really just religious people who do not actually have a personal relationship with God. There are also a great many people who are genuine Christians but who are also religious. Such people exist with a mixture of genuine spiritual life combined with ideas and practices that are not rooted in what we can learn from God through reading the New Testament. Given this, is it really surprising that any of us can be hurt, and sometimes hurt grievously, by those who in claiming to be Christians also claim to represent God?

The question that we need to ask is whether it is justifiable to place blame at God's door for the actions, or inactions, of those who claim to serve him. Surely the answer has to be that this is not warranted. God has given everyone free-will; becoming a Christian doesn't change that. Neither does it stop people from being misguided, selfish, ignorant or arrogant. We need to recognise, and appreciate, the positive changes that God brings about in the lives of those who choose to truly follow him. It is in this that we will actually see the work of God, rather than in the mistakes and mess-ups that God's people still manage to make.

It is Personal

If you are someone who has been hurt by Christians, then please don't let this stop you from finding the truth of God for yourself. Instead, determine in your own heart to try to avoid following other people's examples of bad behaviour. If you have been hurt, then avoid causing similar pain to others. The thing about coming into a relationship with God is that it is personal –it is a personal choice and also a personal relationship. God will work with you, and in you, according to who you are and according to the plans that he has for your life.[2] There is no 'one size fits all'. In fact, no two people are the same, and no two people experience God working in their lives in an identical way. We are all unique in the true sense of the word.

We Get to Choose

Belief in God is based on who he is – his attributes. We each need to embark on a journey of discovery to consider what we can understand about God from the Bible, and to ask him to make himself known to us personally. When he does, then it is 'decision time'. We each come to the point where we are faced with a choice. Do we believe him? Do we trust him? Will we commit ourselves to follow him? We have free-will; we get to choose. The choice we make will have far-reaching consequences. It will set us on a path that determines our destiny for both now and for eternity.

Question 53 – How can I forgive those who have hurt me?

A Big Ask

Forgiveness is hard. Anyone who thinks otherwise has either not been hurt or else doesn't understand what true forgiveness is. Forgiveness entails releasing other people from the consequences of their actions, which is especially difficult to do when the other person has offended us deeply, hurt us or caused us to suffer real loss. Forgiveness is a 'big ask'.

Our Problem

There are two very good reasons for us to forgive others. The first is that we also need forgiveness for the wrong that we do. If we don't, or won't, forgive those who hurt us, why would we expect to receive forgiveness from other people? The second reason is that when we are unforgiving and hold grudges, we ourselves suffer as a result. Often the other party doesn't even realise that they have hurt us, or if they do, they are unlikely to realise the extent of the injury. Even where the offence is clearly understood, the other party may not care; they may simply shrug it off as being our problem, which in a very real sense it is. When we don't forgive, we are holding onto bitterness, even hatred, and we are harmed every day that this continues. Without considering the other party, there is good reason for us to forgive; to do so is in our own best interest.

Trying to Survive

We may readily agree that it would be better for us if we can forgive, but that doesn't change the fact that we have been hurt. Often, we want the person who caused the hurt to suffer, to feel our pain, to realise the full consequence of their actions. The truth is that there are some nasty people out there, but most people aren't like that. Most people are just journeying on the path of life, struggling with their own burdens, trying to make everything work and to survive. Most people don't go out of their way to trip other people up. They don't aim to cause difficulty to others. In fact, they may be surprised and grieved if they learn of the effect that their actions have had.

The Cost

For someone who is a Christian, forgiving others is a little easier than for most other people. This is because Christians have themselves received forgiveness from God. And to receive God's forgiveness requires that we acknowledge, and face up to, our own faults and the consequences of what we have done wrong.[1] There is a cost to us in facing up to our wrongdoing, our sin. But there is also a greater consequence – the price of our forgiveness – the cost to God himself.

Jesus surrendered to an unjust and horrific death in order to pay the penalty of our wrongdoing – mine and yours. Beyond the immense physical agony of crucifixion, Jesus also suffered the pain of separation from God at the point of his death.[2] He accepted this cost to himself in order that we can be forgiven, and through this that we ourselves can enjoy a new and restored relationship with God.

For someone who has received God's forgiveness for all of the bad things that they have done, and who has recognised the price that was paid in order that they can have a relationship with God, it is less hard to release other people.[3] Less hard to let go of hurt and any associated anger and bitterness.[4] But it is still not easy – hurts can go very deep.

Moving On

There are real benefits to forgiving others, both for someone who is a Christian and for someone who is not. Either way, in forgiving others we release ourselves from bitterness; we free ourselves. This enables us to move on.

The Bedroom

Question 54 – What is the Christian view of sex?

Underpinning Everything

Every decision that you make and every action that you take is a reflection of what you believe. This principle applies to each one of us.

For a Christian who is committed to living in a way that pleases God, every thought and every action reflects what they believe about God and about their relationship with him. This includes all areas or life, from the most public to the most personal and intimate. This being the case, it is important when thinking about the Christian faith to also include a perspective on human sexual relationships, and to understand what this means for our thoughts and actions.

Opinions

When the plans for this book were being formulated, a number of people were invited to review the list of topics to be addressed. A few additions were suggested, and subsequently included, but it was also suggested that the present question might be amended to be changed from 'What is the Christian view of sex?' to 'What is God's view of sex?' On the face of it this might seem sensible, except for the fact that we can't speak of something being God's 'view'. Human beings have views; there are many of us and we don't all see things in the same way. The Christian understanding of God is that he is unique, is infinitely wiser and more knowledgeable than any man or woman can ever possibly hope to be, such that it is nonsense to suggest that God has an opinion, a 'view'. If we acknowledge him to be truly God, then anything that he says must be incontrovertible – it must be fact. Consequently, what we are considering within this topic is the Christian understanding of what God has to say about sex, based on what we can learn from the Bible.

Inappropriate?

The starting place must be to emphasise that sex is a very important topic

– to God. It may be that some readers will feel that the inclusion of sex in a book about Christian faith is strange, inappropriate, or even offensive. However, not only is sex an important topic in God's eyes, but it is also very much on the agenda of those who are looking in on Christianity. Many recognise that some sections of the church are confused about the subject of sex and gender. In reality the church has been confused about sex for a long time.

The Roots of Perception

Ancient Greek thought has had a part to play in our understanding of sex. The outlook of the Greeks was that sex is 'of the flesh', unspiritual, dirty. Sadly, the Christian understanding of sex has been tainted by Greek thought, and some parts of the church have embraced the idea of sex as an unfortunate necessity. One might think that the traditional order of service for marriage within the Church of England reflects this when it lists three purposes for marriage. The first relates to the procreation of children, the second to the avoidance of sexual sin, and only lastly comes 'mutual society, help, and comfort'. A more biblical view would put the last first. We can see in the book of Genesis that God's purpose in making woman was to provide a suitable companion for man.[1] There is no mention at that point about procreation or sex, although sex was undoubtedly implicit within this, just as it is in the structure of the male and female bodies.

Let's Enjoy

Marriage, from a Bible perspective, is not so much for the purpose of avoiding sexual sin, as it is the institution that creates the environment for sexual fulfilment and enjoyment. God is very keen to encourage sexual relationships. Anyone who questions this might take a look at the Old Testament book of 'Song of Songs' (also known as 'The Song of Solomon' in some Bible versions). This is a book of love poems that are packed with sexual references, including implicit sexual interactions.

Deep Meaning

Having affirmed that God sees sex very positively, we should take a look at why – understanding this is the crux of the whole discussion about this subject. To comprehend human sexuality from a Bible-based perspective we need to understand that sex was not constructed arbitrarily by God. Neither was it created purely as a mechanism for procreation; human sexual relationship has a deeper meaning than this.

From a spiritual perspective there are direct parallels between the sexual relationship between a man and a woman who are bound together within the marriage covenant, and the relationship between God and the Christian who are bound together in the salvation covenant.[2]

The Big Issue

This is why sex is such an important issue for Christians, and why God has placed the enjoyment of sexual intimacy within the context of marriage – and only within this context. We see this link quite clearly in the understanding of the apostle Paul, as revealed in his New Testament letter to the Ephesians. Here, after describing how a man and woman should relate together within marriage, Paul continues by paralleling this to the relationship between Christ (Jesus) and the church:

> 'For this reason a man will leave his father and mother and be united to his wife, and the two will become one flesh.' This is a profound mystery – but I am talking about Christ and the church.[3]

Paul's teaching on this is all very well, but to be convinced we need something more substantial to grasp hold of and to help with our understanding. So let's get down to specifics and see where the parallels are between the marriage relationship and that which is enjoyed between Christians and God.

Rainbows in the Sky

We don't come across the term 'covenant' very often in everyday life; it is an unfamiliar word to many people. The concept is to be found within legal terminology, and also in the context of marriage – marriage is a covenant made between a man and a woman. The traditional wedding vows form the basis of the marriage covenant. The wedding ceremony is the launch of the lifelong covenant relationship. The Bible mentions a number of covenants that God made with mankind. One of them was made with Noah as representative man. We are told that God made this covenant after he had flooded the earth to destroy everything except for Noah's family and the animals that joined them in the ark – God made a covenant with Noah promising that he would not flood the earth again.[4] As a reminder of this covenant God gave the rainbow[5] – a symbol of promise that we may see in the sky periodically, reminding us that although God sends us rain, he has declared that this will not result in the earth being flooded again.

The Unlocking

The last of the covenants that God made with mankind is known as the 'New Covenant'. The basis of this covenant is Jesus' sacrifice that he made in the place of mankind, forging a way for us to be forgiven by God and to be made acceptable to him.[6] Just as joining together within a marriage covenant unlocks the door for a man and a woman to embark upon an intimate sexual relationship, so the New Covenant opens the way for us to embark upon a new, intimate relationship with God.

Exclusivity

The marriage covenant is by nature an exclusive relationship; its most intimate expression is conducted in privacy, excluding all others. Similarly, the Christian's relationship with God is an exclusive one. Christians may express their worship of God in the presence of others, but the relationship is personal and intimate; their response to God is as deep and exclusive as that of a man and wife. Some may point out that whilst the relationship with God is exclusive from the human side, surely God relates similarly to multitudes of Christians. This is of course true, but while God can have similar relationships with others, this does not diminish his relationship with each individual – Christians do not share their relationship with God; it is not a group relationship but an individual, exclusive, one. What Christians do share is the experience of having such a relationship, which is what brings Christians together to be the church – God's people. This parallel between the two types of relationship is reflected in various passages in the New Testament, where the image of the 'bride' is used to indicate the church, Jesus being the bridegroom.[7]

Commitment

Commitment is something that many find challenging today. There is a general reluctance to commit; we want to take the benefits, but without ties. We see this most strikingly in the social changes in the western world related to relationships. It is as though people want the benefits up-front, and only consider making a commitment as a possible subsequent step. This is definitely not how God intended things to be between men and women, and it is certainly not the way that our relationship with God works. [8] Relationship with God is based on commitment. Before making that commitment we may sense God's presence in some way, but actual relationship only comes about through our submitting to him – our committing ourselves to him. This is illustrated by the teaching of Jesus who states that: *"Whoever believes and is baptised will be saved, but whoever does not believe will be condemned."* [9] In this verse, commitment to God is demonstrated through the physical act of being baptised; an outward act that demonstrates what has happened spiritually. [10]

The Contract

Some religious people like to think that we can drift into having a relationship with God, but this isn't the case. Somewhere or other in our experience there needs to be a decision of our heart and will. This relationship has similarities to a contract – it is only when it is signed by both parties, and duly witnessed and exchanged, that the new contract comes into force. It is only then that the benefits that accrue from the contract become available to the contracting parties. In the spiritual analogy, the benefit for us is forgiveness for all of our wrongdoing, and the opportunity to experience an intimate, personal, spiritual relationship with God.

Parallels

Earlier under this topic we referred to one aspect of the traditional words of the Church of England marriage service. Right at the start of that service there is an acknowledgement of the parallels between marriage and our relationship with God, with the words: "...to join together this man and this woman in holy matrimony ... signifying to us the mystical union that is between Christ and his Church ..."

There are many places in the Bible where our relationship with God is paralleled with that of man and woman within marriage. This is not a merely poetic parallel between the two covenant relationships. If we base our understanding upon what we read in the Bible, then we must surely recognise that the likening of the two covenants with each other is infinitely more significant than mere poetic expression. This is why the current debate over human sexuality is important for Christians. It is not a debate about rights, preferences or choice. The debate comes down to whether or not we will ignore what God himself tells us about human sexuality, and how he intends for us to express it.

Question 55 – Why does the church seem to be hung-up about sex?

Without Excuse

We cannot ignore or escape from the fact that we reside within a cultural context. In fact, from a Christian perspective it is important for the church to engage with culture because this is essential for effective communication of the Christian message. That said, there is no excuse for the church to allow local culture to have an inappropriate influence on its own teaching or practice.

Pax Romana

Christianity came into being at a key point in history when the Roman Empire was at its height. Roman rule had resulted in freedom of movement across the huge expanse of Europe; there was peace, a common language and Roman law and civilisation. This provided an optimal environment for the Christian message to spread far and wide. But, along with it came Greek influence; not just the language, but ideas and to some extent culture as well – and the Christian church was impacted by this, especially in the area of sex. This was in part because of the sexual promiscuity and dissolute behaviour that was evident within the secular culture of the time, and in part because of the Greek philosophical counterbalance to this, which saw sex as something base. These influences were there from the start of Christianity and we see this reflected in some of the comments of the New Testament writers.[1] Paul highlights the contrast between how Christians are meant to behave and the depravity that was evident within the culture of the geographical areas into which the church was expanding.

Reverse Engineering?

The effect of culture on the church is interesting, if sad. Sad because the church ought to be sufficiently well rooted in God as to be able to resist negative influences from the local cultural environment. The Christian theologian Francis Schaeffer, in his book *Escape from Reason*, outlined how change originates with philosophers and then progresses into the arts, then the media, then to popular culture and lastly to the church. At first glance we might see it as negative that the church is last to adopt change, and indeed it is true that change is something that the Christian church tends to be resistant to. However, what is really sad is if the church eventually succumbs to the influence of secular philosophy. Why is this so undesirable? Because the Christian church should be in tune with God and listening to what he says, and as a result ought to exert a positive, godly influence on the society and culture in which it exists. This process should not be working in reverse, as we are experiencing today. We see secular culture influencing the teaching and moral stance of some parts of the church.

Disconnection

Over recent decades we have witnessed an enormous change in how sex is seen and understood within society. This change has effectively disconnected sex from the marriage covenant, from procreation and even from gender. Sex has become little more than a bodily function – one that everyone has the right to experience at any time and in whatever way they feel inclined. This is very different from the view of sex within the Bible as has historically been the perspective of the church. Consequently, the church now finds itself with a tension.

Tension

On the one hand is the traditional, Bible-based appreciation of sex, and on the other hand is the way that sex is currently viewed in secular culture. How Christians respond to this is likely to depend on where they see themselves sitting within the tension that exists between what the Bible tells us and what our culture actually does in practice. This is easier for some parts of the church than others. For some, Christian faith is separate and different to secular culture, with local churches effectively being embassies of God's kingdom and individual Christians being ambassadors of that kingdom.[2] Others tend towards a view of church as the religious wing of the local culture. They feel the pull of that culture and allow it to influence their thinking. This has a direct impact on how sex is viewed by the church.

Church Failure

There are strains between people who see themselves as Christians and feel strongly one way or the other, and those who simply don't see the problem and can't understand what the fuss is all about. The result is an increased focus, and heightened debate between Christians on the issues surrounding sex. Because of the failure of the church generally to fulfil its responsibility to provide spiritual and moral leadership, there is an absence of constraint upon society. As a result, society has marched ahead into a degree of libertinism that has rarely been witnessed before. This leaves a real problem for some Christians, further exaggerating the tensions over sex within the church. The church, as perceived by many looking in from outside, is hung-up about sex.

Uncompromising

This book is about Christian faith and is not aligned to any particular church denomination or grouping; as such there is no pressure to be politically correct, or to steer between views in an effort to avoid controversy. The responses under all 70 topics are entirely founded on what the Bible says and based upon the premise that the Bible is the only basis for genuine Christian faith, and that it forms the baseline for both Christian belief and conduct. Some people deviate from what can be clearly understood from the Bible, either because of religious traditions or because of the pressure of secular culture. Both influences have similar effects; they undermine the Christian message, tending to discredit Christian faith in the eyes of those looking in from the outside, while at the same time grieving the heart of God.

Judgement

One area where society at large is critical of the church, and of individual Christians, is in relation to judgemental attitudes. Some religious people give the impression of thinking themselves to be somehow better than other people. Perhaps due to their own uncertainty about sex, they can be unkindly critical of people whose code of conduct is different to their own. Unkindness is inexcusable and is not a characteristic that Christians have any excuse to adopt. This of course does not mean that truth should be denied, but that where appropriate it should be explained honestly and clearly, but kindly.[3]

Acceptance

For many people discussion about sexual topics is difficult, particularly when looking at them from a moral perspective. In this section – the Bedroom – we are considering what is the Bible-based Christian view about certain sexual practices – behaviours that have now started to be considered to be normal within many western societies. The implication of this is that the Christian, Bible-based view of these things is likely to be different from that of someone looking in at Christianity, someone who may have been living by a secular code in terms of their own sexual conduct. The reader should understand that what is explained within the Bedroom topics is not for one moment intended to be judgemental, but only to explain what the Bible teaches us on these topics.

The church is right to spotlight behaviour that is contrary to what God says is appropriate. But it is also right to show Christian love to those who, for whatever reason, have in the past chosen not to live by God's standards. The message of the Bible is that God's forgiveness is available for everything that we have done in the past, if only we will ask him. Accordingly, the church, and individual Christians, are called to welcome individuals whatever their past.

A Big Difference

Where confusion often occurs is because there is a big difference between someone who is not yet a Christian, and someone who has asked for, and received, God's forgiveness and thereby become a Christian.[4] The Christian, while he or she can yet be forgiven for subsequent wrongdoing, is no longer free to live according to the standards of the world around them. Implicit with asking for God's forgiveness and becoming a Christian is the choice, and commitment, to aim to live in a way that is pleasing to God and consistent with the moral principles that are clearly laid out in the Bible.

Question 56 – Is sex outside of marriage ok?

Being Misunderstood

My wife, Jean, isn't entirely happy when I share this because she thinks that someone may get the wrong idea, but I do sometimes tell people that we have an arranged marriage. I tell them this in all honesty; it is what I actually believe. Our story started with Jean having a conversation with God about whether or not she would be married, as previously related in Question 40. She realised that God may want her to stay single or to be married, and she was content with either. She wanted to know what God's best plan for her was and believed that following his plan would result in the most fulfilling life for her. In the event God made it clear, through something that she read in the Bible, that she would be married.

Jean picked up her conversation with God by asking about whom she would marry and requesting certain characteristics for her future husband. This culminated some weeks later in her seeing me across the room for the first time and being immediately sure that I was the man that God intended for her. Neither of us has any pretentions about this being love-at-first-sight; love for each other had nothing to do with it at this point. Rather it was recognition that I was the man whom God had chosen to be Jean's husband.

It was nearly two years later that I spoke to Jean and learned about this, after I had been on my own journey with God, seeking to know who I should marry (unlike Jean, it didn't really occur to me that I might remain single). Once we both recognised that God had brought us together, we had an 'understanding', even though we were little more than acquaintances. A few months later we became formally engaged to be married; we still didn't know each other at all well, and I at least had a great deal of emotional catching up to do. In fact, the day after asking Jean to marry me, and her responding positively, I wrote her a letter in which I felt compelled to confess that I didn't yet feel 'in love' with her. That didn't go down too well!

The reason why

This story of ours is quite unusual and certainly not the pattern for everyone. The reason I have shared it is to highlight the need to get sex

187

into perspective, into the proper place within relationship. Jean and I were both convinced that God's plan is for sex to be within marriage, and that marriage was to be based on commitment. We also knew that it was important for this commitment to be made in submission to God. Once we knew who we should marry, we were able to commit to each other based on this, rather than on pure emotion or attraction; of course those both grew subsequently, and by the time of our wedding we loved each other very much.

The Big Disconnect

There are all sorts of circumstances upon which people choose to embark upon a sexual relationship. For some, it is convenience; for some, mutual sexual desire or attraction; and for some, genuine love. The Christian perspective is that although love, attraction and desire are all a part of the picture, the basis for a sexual relationship is the covenant of marriage (see the previous two topics). We see this outlined right at the beginning of the Bible where we read God's intention: "That is why a man leaves his father and mother and is united to his wife, and they become one flesh."[1] We have to recognise that for many people this isn't how their story goes; neither is this how things are usually portrayed in films and TV. Here we see sexual relationships occurring as almost the automatic outcome of any man and woman finding themselves thrown together. As viewers we might even have a sense of disappointment if this isn't what the scriptwriter chooses to include. How well the typical media depiction reflects real life for most people is open to debate, but it is beyond question that for the majority of people sex and marriage have, at least in practice, become disconnected.

Definition

Sex outside of marriage can mean a variety of things. For some people it means engaging in sexual encounters before finding the 'right' person to settle down with. For some it means engaging in sex with the person you intend to settle down with, perhaps once engaged to be married. Some people decide to live together without any commitment to eventual marriage. Some people embark on a sexual relationship when they, or the other person, is married to someone else. All of these can be described as sex outside of marriage; they involve sexual intimacy outside of a framework of committed, covenant relationship.

Not Quite Adding Up

We probably ought to take a quick look at marriage at this point. Most people's view of marriage is based on their experience of other people's relationships, especially that of their own parents. Various cultural changes have tended to destabilise marriage as an institution, and the high failure rate doesn't help people to see marriage as the permanent, stable, relationship that it is intended to be – 'till death do us part'. And yet, a large majority of us still want to be married, and for marriage to be a successful, lasting, relationship.

Many people view marriage as a largely legal bond, and if this is your view then you may see the need to marry as more of an administrative convenience than a necessity. But many others still understand marriage to be something more than a legal status. They see it as reflecting something much deeper – a lifelong commitment to be joined together, united in every way. Some people speak of 'saving themselves' till marriage, a preference which is commendable. However, this still doesn't quite add up to the Bible view of marriage; within the Bible, marriage and sexual relationship are integrally bound together, effectively synonymous.

Not to Plan

When we look back at the current question in the light of this, then we have to say that sexual relationships that occur outside of the marriage covenant are not what God intends for us. From a Christian perspective, no sexual relationship other than with the person we are actually married to can be seen as being ok.[2] However, this is not simply a matter of 'rules', and certainly not about taking a judgemental attitude. The message of the Bible is that God has shown us how to live well, how to enjoy life to the full. As much as for any other reason, it is for our wellbeing that God has shown us the appropriate context for sexual relationship within our lives. God wants us to have the best relationship possible; the circumstance which he has designed for this to be fulfilled within is the covenant relationship of marriage.

Question 57 – What does the Bible say about same-sex relationships?

What's the Difference?

In the previous topics in the Bedroom section we have looked at the Christian perspective on sex, and also on sexual relationships that occur outside of marriage. When it comes to same-sex relationships, we find that there are some specific questions to be considered. Firstly, should these relationships be seen in a different way to heterosexual sex that occurs outside of marriage? And secondly, is there any justification for viewing same-sex relationships as in some way better or worse than heterosexual relationships that take place outside of marriage?

Before addressing these questions, we need to be clear that we are taking the biblical view of marriage as between one man and one woman. From this basis, same-sex relationships can only take place outside of the biblical view of marriage and are therefore not ok from a Christian viewpoint.

In that same-sex relationships are anatomically incapable of representing sex as defined for a man and woman (i.e. becoming 'one flesh' as the male and female bodies were designed to do) there cannot be a direct link to a covenant relationship. This could be interpreted as being more acceptable than heterosexual relationships that take place outside of the marriage covenant. However, the Bible makes it abundantly clear that same-sex relationships are contrary to God's design and plan for mankind. In fact, we find that same-sex relationships are condemned in no uncertain terms in the Bible, both in the Old Testament and the New.[1]

Why?

We need to consider why it is that the Bible stance on same-sex relationships is so strong, and we also need to consider what the Christian approach should be towards those who are involved in a so-called 'gay' lifestyle.

In terms of what we can read in the Bible, the simple fact is that the Bible writers are reflecting the heart of God himself. It is not adequate to suggest that ancient culture alone is responsible for the strong opposition to same-sex relationships that we find in the Bible. In fact, if culture has had any influence then it is arguable that the culture itself was formed on the basis of what God had previously shown to his people, starting at the very beginning in the creation story. If we return to the early chapters of the Bible we see that God's plan was for there to be a union between a man and a woman.[2] This is his pattern and any other sexual relationship is a deviation and distortion of this. We might justifiably say that from the perspective of what we find recorded in the Bible, people who engage in other types of sexual relationship are in rebellion against God's pattern, and thereby against God himself.[3]

The 'Creation'

Having concluded that same-sex relationships are not acceptable to God, we move on to ask how Christians should respond when confronted by people who engage in such relationships. During the six months before Jean and I were married, I worked on constructing what was to be our bed. I should explain that I am particularly tall, and we wanted a bed that was extra long. I am also something of a designer, and so wanted what I made to be as good as it could be. The outcome was a bed that was non-standard in features as well as length – a 'creation'. This bed served us for some 33 years, albeit with changes in mattress. Eventually, when we were anticipating moving to a new house again, we decided that it was time to have something new. This decision was partly driven by the fact that my 'creation' was quite complex to take apart and reassemble. We purchased a new kingsize bed, and in spite of the strong emotional attachment, offered our old, and rather special, bed up for auction on eBay. When the buyer arrived to collect his purchase I was pleased to see that, like me, he was tall; he was very enthusiastic about my 'creation' and thrilled that he had won the auction. However, it was equally apparent that the bed was destined for use by him and his male partner. I would have been delighted had the bed gone to a young couple such as Jean and I had been when it was new, but instead was shocked at where it was going, and how it was destined to be used. I even, fleetingly, considered refusing to hand it over, but quickly thought better of it.

God Loves

Later I realised that God was teaching me something through this rather tender experience. The lesson being that while God certainly condemns same-sex relationships, his love is still there for the people who are involved in this lifestyle. It is this understanding that Christians should be mindful of – God hates sin, but he loves people and wants them to come to him and receive forgiveness and reconciliation.[4]

Clear Thinking

Christians need to show understanding towards people who don't claim to be Christians and who live in a way that the Bible shows us is wrong in God's eyes – whatever sin this involves. After all, every Christian was living in ways that were not pleasing to God prior to their becoming Christians.[5] Having said this, the church should be clear about its opposition to any celebration or promotion of sinful lifestyles, or cultures. There is a momentum within the popular media that is portraying alternate sexual lifestyles as normal, wholesome or healthy, whereas the message of the Bible is that they are anything but. This inverting of reality – reengineering of truth – is something that the Old Testament book of Isaiah warns about where it states:

> Woe to those who call evil good and good evil,
> who put darkness for light and light for darkness,
> who put bitter for sweet and sweet for bitter.[6]

The inversion of truth is nothing new. It is just that we are experiencing this in a particular way at the present time. Those who are Christians are called by God to recognise the current trend for what it is and respond in ways that are pleasing to him.

Question 58 – What is the Christian view of transgender?

Stereotypes

Within the topic 'Are men and women equal?' (Q 13) we considered the fact that a great many of us don't fit neatly within the cultural gender stereotypes such as were depicted by Hollywood for much of the 20th century. When thinking about men and women we need to have a realistic understanding of what differentiates us, rather than a perspective based on some artificial depiction of something that purports to be the 'ideal'. Only a small minority of men would fit easily within the stereotype of the Hollywood he-man; similarly, most women are nothing like the Barbie doll image.

The reality is that within both sexes there is a range of characteristics: body shapes, facial features, hair colour, emotional make-up, temperament, etc. It would suit some people if we were to think of these differences as being a single continuum, with the stereotypes at either end, and the vast majority of us being somewhere between the two. But most of us would agree that such a 'gender scale' is counter intuitive. They would assert that 'no', we are male or we are female, whilst at the same time recognising that there are variations within both sexes. This accords with what we can read in the Bible:

> *So God created mankind in his own image,*
>
> *in the image of God he created them;*
>
> *male and female he created them.*
>
> *God blessed them and said to them, "Be fruitful and increase in number ..."* [1]

In saying this God depicted gender identities very clearly; there are females who bear children and males who sire children.

Exceptions

It is very important to recognise here that, whilst we are clear that God made us to be either male or female, a very small minority of people are born with a condition that is referred to as 'intersex'. This is where the body has not formed normally and the gender is unclear from the external genitalia. The present topic is not intended to cover this area of gender confusion, but we do need to acknowledge it, and to state that this is something entirely different to our consideration of transgender. Individuals, and their families, who find themselves needing to face the challenges associated with this condition surely deserve to receive the utmost understanding and support from us all.

Deceptive Appearances

People who think of themselves as transgender are those who were born, and subsequently developed, with typical male or female anatomies and characteristics, but who feel that they were born with 'the wrong body'. We would therefore conclude that the desire to identify as the opposite gender has an emotional and/or psychological basis rather than a physical one, and that it is on this level that the person concerned is in need of help and support. The Bible is quite clear-cut when it comes to gender; apart from acknowledging the existence of eunuchs, the only Bible passage that seems to relate specifically to the question of transgender is found in the Old Testament where we read: "A woman must not wear men's clothing, nor a man wear women's clothing, for the Lord your God detests anyone who does this."[2] Some people may choose to argue about exactly what this means, but what it says is clear – a man is a man and a woman is a woman; their behaviour and their appearance should reflect what God has made them to be.

Let's be Absolutely Clear

We live in a world where absolutes are not fashionable. Unfortunately, some parts of the church have readily allowed themselves to be sucked into embracing this 'flexible' worldview, but it is not one that is in any way supported by what we can read in the Bible; it is not one that is endorsed by God. God's message to us today is the same as it has always been: it is one of absolutes – blacks and whites, not greys. God has made us male and female and wants us to enjoy being who he has made us. No matter what we have done in the past, or have deliberately permitted others to do to us, the message of the Bible is that God's love is there for everyone.[3] He wants us to recognise and embrace the truth about ourselves, and to approach him asking for forgiveness, cleansing and a new life lived according to his plan.[4]

Question 59 – Why do some church leaders abuse children?

Spotlight

There are two issues that relate to child abuse that is perpetrated by religious leaders. The first is the actual abuse; the second relates to the institutional cover-up of these acts.

The matter of cover-up is the simplest to address. Some time ago Jean and I made one of our infrequent visits to the cinema. We chose to watch the film 'Spotlight', which is about the true-life investigation by the Boston Globe newspaper into allegations of child sexual abuse within the Catholic Church. It wasn't what you might call a 'fun' film, but it was moving. I particularly enjoy films about courage and fighting for what is right, and this is precisely what the Spotlight team set about to do. It seems that the large-scale abuse and cover-up that the Spotlight team exposed within the city of Boston, Massachusetts, was only the tip of the iceberg. This is a tragic story about acts that devastated the lives of the victims and seriously undermined confidence in the Catholic Church.

Negative Publicity

We can only assume that where cover-up occurs it is because the particular institution is afraid of the impact of negative publicity; this is entirely understandable, although just as unacceptable. Child abuse is not only despicable and immoral, but also illegal in most countries. No religious institution can justify thinking itself to be above such a law.

Mistaken Compassion

Another reason why cover-up might occur is out of compassion for the perpetrator. Churches do sometimes place the feelings or sensitivities of individuals above the common good, not to mention above the honour of God – and this extends much more widely than sexual sin alone. So, although sensitivity is required in handling these situations, wrongdoing must be addressed appropriately, and the consequences faced up to by the perpetrator and also the institution or group that they represent.[1]

It is pertinent here to discuss reasons why abuse may happen in a church situation, understanding that this includes any type of sexual impropriety perpetrated by people in a position of authority

Weakness

This first point to be made is certainly not intended as an excuse but is a statement of reality. This point is that we are all weak and vulnerable to impulses to behave wrongly – to thoughts and actions that the Bible refers to as 'sin'.[2] Becoming a Christian does not remove the inclination to sin, but it should involve a change within the person's heart, causing them to make a commitment to live in a way that will please God. Consequently, Christians have a high standard to live up to, and God provides the ability for them to do so; however, we are weak human beings and can still fail to live as we should.[3]

Pretending

Secondly, it is wrong to assume that everyone who purports to be a Christian leader is necessarily a Christian in more than name. A long time ago when training at Bible College, I was part of a small group of students who were invited to take a service at the local Salvation Army Citadel (Church). During a conversation with the officer in charge I asked whether all Salvation Army officers were actually Christians. Although this was a long time ago, I remember the response clearly; he said that he "would like to think so". The clear inference was that whilst they certainly should be, his experience made him think that maybe not all were. The point here is that we should, quite rightly, expect a high standard of behaviour from Christians, and even more so from anyone who takes on a church leadership role. However, where someone's 'Christianity' is actually only 'religiousness', they will not have the personal relationship with God that empowers real Christians to live in a way that pleases God and brings honour to his name.[4] The apostle Paul has left us with clear instructions about the moral and spiritual qualifications that must be met by those being considered for church leadership roles.[5] Obviously, if Paul's guidance is not followed then this places the church at risk.

Sexless Lifestyle

The third point is that instances of sexual abuse by church leaders seem more frequently to occur within the context of what is supposed to be a celibate lifestyle. Celibacy means to living a life that doesn't involve any sexual relationship. We must recognise that being single is equally valid to being married; the apostle Paul was himself single and celibate, and advocated this for some people.[6] However, it is a fundamental error for churches to mandate celibacy for those who hold office. The Bible, early in the book of Genesis, makes it clear that God recognised that Adam was alone and needed a mate, someone who was like Adam and who would complement him, comfort him and support him. In order to meet Adam's need, God created Eve. The bonding of a man and a woman, to travel the path of life together, is the only context in which God intends sexual intimacy to take place. It seems obvious that to mandate celibacy for religious leaders means that they may be more vulnerable to temptation. Again, this is not an excuse for the individual perpetrator, but perhaps an aggravating circumstance that serves to heighten the temptation towards seriously inappropriate acts of sexual and emotional gratification.

Question 60 – Is marriage the only option?

Options

The pattern that God has given us for sexual relationship is that this is to be expressed exclusively within the context of marriage. But that clearly doesn't mean that everyone should marry; there is another path.

Being Celibate

Western culture has become highly sexualised to the extent that sex is viewed as a bodily function that deserves to be satisfied, irrespective of our relationship status. Consequently, celibacy tends to be seen by many as a strange decision, even when this is taken in anticipation of eventual marriage. This perception is exaggerated where someone makes a life choice to be celibate. But we need to recognise that either of these decisions is at least as valid as other sexual choices, and that each person has the absolute right to choose their own path. Celibacy is a good path to choose and is God's intention for everyone unless, and until, they marry.

Being Single

For some people, remaining single is a conscious decision that, rather than committing their energy and resources to marriage and potentially to supporting a family, they will use their lives to make a difference in other ways. The apostle Paul himself made this decision and was an advocate for the benefits of the single life.[1] But we must recognise that for many people, being single is less of a choice and more circumstantial; they would like to marry, and hope that their current status is a temporary one.

We all start out single and, whatever our marital status may become, life for each one of us will end when we die and face our Maker as "me" rather than as half of "us".[2] There are, of course, circumstances in which someone who has been married will return to living as a single person later on. This may be for different reasons, each presenting its own difficulties. For most this will be a decisive change, through death or marriage breakup. However, some people find themselves continuing to be married but required to live without their partner due to illness or disability, military service or imprisonment, etc.

Decisions

God has a plan for each person. The key to living a meaningful and fulfilled life is to commit to his plan. Firstly, this entails grasping hold of his offer of forgiveness and a new start (see the 'The Contract' section). But then it involves entering into a close relationship with God and following his guidance.[3] He loves us and wants the best for us. We need to trust him and commit to following wherever he leads us, including whether we will be single or married. Whichever state we find ourselves in today, God's intention is that we should embrace it. We might anticipate something different for the future, but we should surely make the most of the present and the opportunities that our current situation provides for us.

Forerunners

We are not necessarily told which Bible characters were single and which were married, however we do know this for some. We have already mentioned Paul. The other major character within the New Testament who was undoubtedly single was Jesus himself. From a Bible perspective it is clear that marriage is not the path for everyone, and that being single can afford opportunities that marriage does not. Just consider what Jesus accomplished, and the extensive and fruitful missionary enterprise that Paul engaged in.[4]

True Community

The Christian church has always recognised the place and contribution of those living the single life. In times past this may have been worked out through convents or the monastic system. The increased liberty that we all enjoy today means that each person is free to choose to live in whatever status they believe God has called them to, whether individually or within a family unit.

Churches often have a focus upon supporting families, but this is not to sideline those who are single; the church is there to encourage and support each individual irrespective of their marital status. The local church is, after all, a community – a very special one in which every member has an important, valuable, God-given part to play.

The Roof

Question 61 – Why do bad things happen?

Frame of Reference

Any honest attempt to provide answers to the questions that are asked about Christian faith has to address this topic, but it is almost certainly the hardest response to make. That is not to imply that there is no answer, but only that the answer is not a simple one. The only reasonable explanations as to why bad things happen require the reader to be willing to consider the issue from God's perspective, and not simply from the perspective of those who suffer. If this is you then please read on.

Suffering is not Ok

There is no point in pretending that any of us is ok with tragedy, loss, disappointment or stress. They hurt us and challenge our confidence, in whomever that confidence may be based – ourselves, some other person, or God. There are two responses to such events: the first is how we cope with the circumstances at the time; the second is what we see as being the cause of our suffering. Although the first of these is hugely significant for us, it is the second response that the current topic is focussed on, and which is ultimately the more important.

Tragedies

Let's start by thinking about the sort of tragedies that can befall us. You can probably identify with one or more of these. There are the obvious ones that cause death, injury and life-changing disruption on a large scale, such as military conflict, earthquakes and other natural disasters. Then there are the smaller scale but no less devastating tragedies, such as road accidents, industrial accidents, murder, rape, and other criminal acts. Finally, there are the more common types of struggle such as untimely death, relationship breakdown, loss of employment, disability or debilitating illness, miscarriage or childlessness. All of these leave us asking the profound question 'Why?'

Having accepted the premise that we need to see these tragic events from God's perspective, first let us briefly think about the differences between the two perspectives: ours and God's.

Our Perspective

As human beings we have a very strong instinct for self-preservation; generally speaking we don't want to die, and we will go to great lengths to stay alive. Most of us also do whatever we can to stay healthy, safe and secure. We have a tendency to do what is in our personal interest, to seek gratification for our own desires, and to promote our own wellbeing through acquiring and retaining wealth. We also like to be noticed and valued, and we tend to shun judgement from other people. We are reluctant to accept criticism. We are inclined towards selfishness; our world view tends to place ourselves at the centre.

Think about it – is this harsh or is it realistic? We aren't totally selfish, but all of us are selfish in part.

Gods Perspective

God made the whole of the creation, and he made us to fulfil his high purpose through having a relationship with himself. Initially mankind did have a relationship with God, and he set the first people in a beautiful place where life was easy.[1] In spite of this, it didn't take very long before our ancestors rebelled against God. As a result, he changed our environment to one where we would experience the struggle of adversity and through this be disciplined.[2] This was to keep mankind from being corrupted totally. Since then God has wooed us continually through providing aid to us and sending his messengers to help us to understand his hopes and plans for us. Eventually, because mankind still didn't follow his ways, God sent his own Son, Jesus, to become a human being.[3] Jesus came to make a way for us to be reconciled to God, in order to achieve this he submitted to an unjust, horrific and degrading execution.[4] Jesus stands as a towering example of one who has suffered 'bad things' happening.

Think about it – God has done everything to meet our needs and to encourage us to have a relationship with himself. He continues to woo us even today.

Now that we have taken a reality check, we are ready to look at how to answer that question: "Why?"   The roof of a house usually consists of multiple surfaces that work together to provide an overall covering and protection for the structure below. The following set of propositions mirror the house roof; they are intended to work together to provide an overall answer to why bad things happen.

Proposition 1

Each of us lives our life as we see best, making decisions based on circumstances. Sometimes we make decisions from wrong motives or based on a failure to think through the potential consequences. Sometimes we are overly optimistic or allow ourselves to be misled by our own hearts or by the influence of others. Whatever the reason, there are consequences to our actions (or inactions), and we are ultimately to blame for these.

If a gambling habit results in someone having no money, then they may try to place the responsibility for this onto the lottery number selectors, the horse or the football team, or for that matter the bookie. In the cold light of day however, they will know that it is themselves that are responsible, and that they will have to cope with any adverse impact resulting from their choices.

Very often the consequences of our wrongdoing affect other people as well as ourselves; ie. the gambler's wife, children and even extended family. There are of course other scenarios where the guilty party may suffer little, but where there are victims of their action who suffer greatly. We tend to see this as unfair. But just as our own choices have implications for us, so the choices of other people impact us. This reminds us that we have all been spoiled as a result of mankind's rebellion against God. Normally we get by without being confronted by our human failings, but tragic events underline just how flawed we are, and how much we need to be restored into relationship with God.

- Bad things happen as a consequence of human selfishness.

Proposition 2

Many circumstances can result in untimely death: war, natural disaster, terrorist attacks, road accidents, serious illness, etc. Sudden death is a huge challenge to us because it conflicts with our instinct to survive. For many people the very idea of death is difficult, perhaps because we can't cope with the idea of a life being expired, of that person's existence being gone forever. Or, it may be that we think that there is a life after death, but fear what that might be like; the unknown frightens us.

Like ripples on a pond, tragic death impacts other people. There is bereavement of course, but also the need to adjust our lives to cope without the one who has died. If we look beyond this impact, do we take death too seriously? Is it such a big deal? We can be sure that the life we enjoy now will end, some day. If there is no God, no heaven and no hell, if death is the ultimate end, then there are no consequences for us when we die and there is nothing to fear. Conversely, if the message of the Bible is true then our future beyond the grave depends on the choice we have made during our lifetime. Someone has said that if we don't choose to have a relationship with God now, why would we want one when we die?

- Bad things happen to remind us that life is fleeting, and we have a choice to make.

Proposition 3

So often we get on with our lives with a focus on the 'now', or at least on the foreseeable future. In doing so we probably rely on our personal resources: our physical prowess, appearance, aptitude, skill, specialist knowledge, career, etc. But God wants us to have a broader perspective, to recognise that he has made us for a higher purpose than what we alone can achieve in the 'now'. God has made us to fulfil his purposes during our lives, and for a future life beyond our earthly existence. To this end God sometimes allows us to be confronted by our frailty, or to lose the basis for our security. To us this can be devastating, but where God allows this to happen it is because he wants to open our eyes to something beyond ourselves – to him and his love for us, and his higher purposes for our lives.

- Bad things happen to encourage us to see beyond ourselves.

Proposition 4

Athletes have always trained to build up bodily strength, suppleness and endurance. But we know that there is more to success within the sporting arena than pure physical prowess. We realise that to be the best they can be, athletes need to train their minds as well as their bodies. This training of the mind entails disciplined focus, but also the management of emotions. Athletes need to be able to minimise the effect of adversity on their performance – we may think of this as building character.

Character is about virtues such as courage, fortitude, honesty and faithfulness. For an athlete this entails pressing through the pain barrier and giving their very best, irrespective of what may have gone before. For every one of us God is interested in character. In fact, character is so important to God that he provides circumstances that will enable our character to develop, and also circumstances to prove our character. Often these circumstances are difficult for us – which is why they are useful for character building.

- Bad things happen so that our character can be strengthened.

Proposition 5

On the 8th of November 1987, in Enniskillen, Northern Ireland, at the height of what came to be known as 'the Troubles', the IRA exploded a terrorist bomb near the town's war memorial during a Remembrance Day ceremony. Eleven people lost their lives at the time, and sixty-three others were injured; a twelfth person was to die after spending thirteen years in a coma. This event deserves to be listed as a tragedy if anything does, but out of this intense darkness a bright light shone. The bomb blew out the wall of a building, burying people in the rubble, including a father and daughter, Gordon and Marie Wilson; Marie died in hospital later that day.

A few hours after the bombing, when interviewed by the BBC, Gordon

Wilson declared his forgiveness for the terrorists who had killed his daughter, saying that he would pray for them. Gordon's astonishing act of forgiveness was reported and taken note of right around the world, and for many people is forever linked with the memory of that event. For all who are willing to see, that heroic act of forgiveness demonstrates what we have been discussing in this book; that God is for real and lives are changed when people are committed to following him.

- Bad things happen so that God can be glorified through our response.

Proposition 6

You may be familiar with the slightly dated expression 'the patience of Job'. This man Job (pronounced *Jobe*) is a character in the Bible who endured total personal disaster, a case of 'bad things happening' in a big way. Job's story is recorded in the book of Job in the Old Testament part of the Bible. Job worshipped God and was blameless and upright. He was also a very wealthy man, a billionaire in his day. The Bible tells us about a conversation in heaven, where Satan (the devil) claimed that Job only worshiped God because God blessed him with wealth, and that if this was taken from him then Job would surely curse God.[5]

In response God put everything that Job possessed into Satan's hands, enabling him to take it away from Job. So Satan caused all of Job's possessions and children to be lost in a single day. After some time, when Job continued to honour God, there was a second conversation with God in which Satan claimed that if God afflicted Job in his body, then Job would curse God.[6] Again, in response to this God permitted Satan to afflict Job with skin sores from head to toe. Even Job's wife told him to 'curse God and die', but Job would not give way. Later in the book of Job we see him saying, "though He (God) slay me, yet will I trust in Him."[7] This story suggests to us that sometimes 'bad' things happen to us because of the work of Satan. Just as in the story of Job we need to understand that although Satan is against us, God will not permit us to be pushed beyond what we are capable of enduring.

- Bad things happen because of the acts of Satan.

Proposition 7

Jonah was known as a prophet. His story is recorded in the book of Jonah in the Old Testament. A prophet was someone who God communicated with, revealing his purposes to them. Prophets were then expected to share what they heard from God with the people for whom the message was intended – in this case the people of the great city of Nineveh. God wanted to tell the people of Nineveh to change their ways and worship him. The problem was that Jonah didn't want this commission to Nineveh. The people there were enemies of his own people, and Jonah knew that if he did what God wanted then they would change their ways and avoid the punishment that Jonah felt they deserved.

So Jonah ran away, taking passage on a ship that was headed in the opposite direction to Nineveh. God decided to stop Jonah from thwarting his plan and to get him back on track to perform the task he had given him. As a result, God arranged for Jonah to be thrown overboard by the ship's crew, and then to be swallowed by a 'big fish'.[8] When inside the fish, Jonah was struck with guilt for disobeying God, and prayed to ask for God's help. In response to this prayer God caused the fish to vomit Jonah onto dry land. Then God reminded Jonah of the commission he had given to him to speak to the people of the city of Nineveh. This time Jonah actually did as God asked him to, albeit very reluctantly. The outcome was that the people of Nineveh responded positively to God's message via Jonah, and in doing so avoided God's punishment. Sometimes we have to undergo difficulty for the ultimate benefit of others.

- Bad things happen to achieve God's higher purposes for us and/or the world.

❖ **Question 62 – Does God care about human suffering?**

Jesus Wept

The only place to find an answer to this question is in the Bible, which helpfully sums up how God feels about suffering in one verse. The shortest verse in the Bible, found in the Gospel according to John, reads very simply: "Jesus wept."[1] This verse and the context in which it appears correspond exactly to what we have thought about in the previous question when considering why 'bad things' happen. In this Bible story, Jesus' friend Lazarus was ill. Yet Jesus deliberately kept away even though he knew that Lazarus was about to die. Jesus arrived at the home of his friend some time afterwards, when Lazarus' body had already been in his tomb for four days. The point is that Jesus had the power to have healed Lazarus while he was still alive, and also had the power to raise him from the dead, even after four days. And yet Jesus' heart was still tender to the suffering of Lazarus himself, the bereavement of his two sisters whom he had lived with, and to the mourning of the community. And so we read that Jesus wept with them in their grief. Even when Jesus went to the tomb for the express purpose of raising Lazarus back to life, we read that Jesus was "once again deeply moved."[2] Jesus knew the end from the beginning; he knew that he was about to perform a wonderful miracle, to raise Lazarus back to life, and yet he was still sensitive to human suffering.

Substitute

Not only is God sensitive to our suffering, but he is also willing to suffer in our place. Jesus' life was anything but easy, and the three years that he was actively ministering was clouded by the opposition of unscrupulous men. But this was nothing to the physical suffering that surrounded his death, as was dramatically depicted in Mel Gibson's film 'The Passion of the Christ'. However, even this physical suffering was dwarfed by what was happening in the spiritual realm. Here we see Jesus taking upon himself the weight of sin of the whole world – the Living Bible version, in the first letter of John, puts it this way:

> *He is the one who took God's wrath against our sins upon himself*

and brought us into fellowship with God; and he is the forgiveness for our sins, and not only ours but all the world's. [3]

In doing this Jesus' relationship with God was temporarily broken, causing him to exclaim from the cross where he died: "My God, my God, why have you forsaken me?"[4] We cannot possibly imagine the pain that the rift in this relationship entailed for Jesus, for God, or for the whole community of heaven.

The End

We have a promise from God for the future, referring to how things will be in heaven. In the New Testament book of Revelation, at the end of the Bible, we read:

> *He will wipe every tear from their eyes. There will be no more death or mourning or crying or pain, for the old order of things has passed away.* [5]

Here God reminds us that what we experience now is transitory - we have hope for the future. He is sensitive to our suffering; he clearly does not take this lightly.

The Garden

 ## Question 63 – How should I react to the news headlines?

Nothing New

The writer of the book of Ecclesiastes in the Old Testament part of the Bible states rather despondently, "What has been will be again, what has been done will be done again; there is nothing new under the sun."[1] This was written some 3000 years ago, and yet it rings true for us today. Yes, we have new technologies that enable us to do things that weren't possible previously, but in essence even these new opportunities are not new and not really different. Today we are exploring the universe, but mankind has always explored and discovered new things and new places.

The same applies in the area of turmoil, conflict and disasters; these have always existed. The only real difference is that today we tend to know what is happening very quickly and have the possibility of knowing everything that is happening in the world, not just those things that are local to our own community. The news headlines can feel overwhelming, frightening and depressing. Sometimes as individuals we can have a small influence on events, but mostly we have none at all; we have no control of what is happening in the world around us and can feel threatened by the decisions and actions of other people.

Perspectives

So, what is the Christian take on the world around, and the events that make the headlines? We need to recognise that there are two perspectives here; there is the general perspective, which applies for everyone, and then there is the perspective that applies for the person who has placed their life in God's hands. Let's start by looking at the general perspective.

Good Advice

As a young man I worked for a few years in the family business with my dad. Although I look back on this as a valuable time in many ways, working with my dad wasn't easy; in fact it caused me serious stress at times. At one point I felt so affected by this that I consulted my family doctor to see if there was something that he could give me to help with the symptoms of this stress. He didn't prescribe medication, but instead gave me some advice which I have never forgotten. He said that if I had the opportunity to change the circumstances that were causing the stress then I should do so, otherwise I needed to accept the circumstances and stop resisting them. I think that this doctor's advice is pertinent here: we should work to apply whatever influence we have available to us for changing the world for the better, but where we have no influence we need simply to accept that this is how things are. In the Gospel according to Matthew, in the New Testament, Jesus asks, "Can any one of you by worrying add a single hour to your life?[2]" That chapter ends with some other words of Jesus: "Therefore do not worry about tomorrow, for tomorrow will worry about itself. Each day has enough trouble of its own."[3]

Assurance

Those who have put their lives in God's hands know that they can trust him in whatever circumstances they are confronted with, and whatever hardship they may face. They are assured of God's love for them – that he is 'for them'.[4] Not only that, but they also know that God has a purpose for their life; it has meaning.[5] There is a God-given direction to be followed, and there will be a worthwhile outcome. This is not just wishful thinking; it is what the Bible tells us.[6] More importantly, it is what the Spirit of God witnesses to in the hearts of those who have committed their lives to obeying God.[7]

Question 64 – What is life about?

Something to Contemplate

This is a pertinent question, no matter which stage of life we happen to be in. It may not be something that we ask ourselves often, but perhaps only in those quiet moments of thoughtfulness and contemplation. For me, graveyards have always been poignant places. When I was a young child living in Isleworth in west London, there was a graveyard that we used to walk past. It was rather an unkempt place. Many of the headstones leaned strangely, the graves seemed to be scattered across the ground in haphazard fashion, and the grass was untended and dishevelled. In my young mind I wondered about the lives of those long-departed people and what, if anything, remained to mark their existence beyond those stark memorial stones. In the book of Psalms, in the Old Testament part of the Bible, the psalmist writes: "Lord, what are human beings that you care for them, mere mortals that you think of them? They are like a breath; their days are like a fleeting shadow."[1]

Hope

For many, the busyness of life drowns out such thoughts, but for some people it is the humdrum grind that itself brings questions to mind. What is it all for? What can I hope for in future?

We could think about the 'deeper things of life' such as relationships with family and community which can give our lives great meaning. But our real purpose is based on our being in relationship with God; without this relationship and the hope that it brings, we have no truly satisfying answer. The message that we see very clearly in the Bible is that there is meaning to life for every one of us, whatever our immediate circumstances. God has formed us for a purpose. In the New Testament letter to the Romans we read: "And we know that in all things God works for the good of those who love him, who have been called according to his purpose."[2]

God created us to live in relationship with himself; it is part of who we are.

It should not surprise us that we feel incomplete when we do not have this relationship, that at times our lives feel empty or directionless, without satisfying meaning.

Achievement

Most of us have aspirations and find satisfaction in our striving to achieve these. But ultimately the things that we aim for, and value, are in themselves fleeting. My father-in-law was strongly motivated to serve other people and to help make their lives better. Although his job was not prestigious (he worked a machine on the factory floor) he became the president of his trade union, and also chairman of the local council. These things had particular meaning for his life. But once he retired, experienced ill health and was no longer active in these roles, his contribution became just a memory; everyone else seemed to move on and to have forgotten him. It is only through being in relationship with God that our lives have a meaning that is both complete and eternal.

He has a Plan

When I was seventeen years old I was a regular churchgoer, and assumed that this meant that I was a Christian. Through talking with others who were Christians I learned that relationship with God is a conscious decision, and not something that one can absorb by attending church. I was told that God loved me, that he had a purpose for my life, and that he would forgive me for the things that I had done wrong. For some people it is a sense of guilt or shame that draws them to God. They have the sense of needing forgiveness, of needing to be washed clean. Although this certainly did apply for me, the thing that most drew me was the thought that God had a purpose and a plan for my life. There was a choice to be made; whether to continue 'doing my own thing' or to commit to following God's purpose for me.[3] This choice applies for every one of us. The invitation is there – we each need to make this decision for ourselves.

Question 65 – How can my life be better?

Comical Misrepresentation

When I started to write this book, I submitted the initial idea to a small number of contacts to ask for feedback. One of those I invited to comment is the son of a friend, a teenager who had declared himself to be an atheist. Although disappointed, I wasn't surprised when this young man declined my invitation; I was, however, taken aback by the reason he gave. He apparently believes that Christian faith is all about going to heaven when you die, which he seems to think is fanciful. The thing is that this common perception is a caricature of what Christian faith is all about, like one of those drawings of a person with a disproportionately large head and exaggerated facial features – a comical misrepresentation. At first, I was perplexed by this young man's comment because it couldn't be more different to my own experience and perception. For me, being a Christian is very much about the now, albeit there is certainty of a future life as well. Sadly, there are some religious people who live as though they are in some sort of holding pen, waiting for fulfilment after death. But this couldn't be further from the truth. Christian faith speaks very clearly indeed about the lives that we live now, addressing the question of how our lives can be better.

To Change or not to Change ...

One of the attributes of God is that he does not change; in theological terms it is said that God is 'immutable'. There are two apparent ironies here, the first being that God who does not change is in the 'change business'. His purpose for us here on earth is that we change. Those things about us that are an expression of our corrupted nature should be cast off and replaced with good and wholesome things that reflect how God himself is, and how he intended us to be when he made us. God is in the business of enabling this change and also helping us to apply change in our lives. The second irony is that while God is in the change business, churches tend to resist change. They can appear to be frozen in time, like a historic snapshot, transfixed. Given that God is in the change business, knowing him can make our lives better. This is outlined below under three headings: Relationship, Prayer and Pattern.

Relationship

Relationship with God is a general theme that runs through this book. This is because relationship is the essence of what Christian faith is about; it is coming into a relationship with God, and continuing our lives in relationship with him. Apart from anything else, we were designed to have this relationship and we are spiritually bereft without it. Coming into this relationship entails receiving forgiveness for all those things that we have allowed ourselves to think, feel and do, that are at odds with how God designed us to be – receiving forgiveness for our 'sin'. It is impossible to overemphasise the significance of this forgiveness. Guilt is such a binding thing, such a divisive thing, so isolating – God offers us freedom from this through the forgiveness that Jesus made possible. But in some respects, forgiveness is the negative part about coming into a relationship with God; it is about recovering from what has gone on before. The bigger part is the 'now'. Having a relationship with God enables us to know his purpose for us now, today, and to achieve that purpose by the strength that he will give us.

Prayer

The Bible describes God as a father. A relationship with God is a lot like that of a father and child. This is not to suggest that we remain infants in this relationship, or that we should be 'childish'. When our children were born, Jean and I had a very clear sense that they were on loan to us, and that our role was to help them to mature and to become independent people who were equipped to face the life that they would lead. This doesn't mean that now they are adults we no longer have a relationship, or that they no longer need or rely on us for anything; in fact, our son and daughter-in-law who recently returned to the UK from Australia are currently living in our home with us.

The point is that having a relationship with God has privileges attached. One of my favourite books in the Old Testament part of the Bible is the book of Esther. Esther married the king of Persia, Xerxes. When a Persian king was seated in his throne room, even his wife could not approach him without being summoned.[1] In the story of Esther, circumstances arise such that Esther needed to take her life in her hands and risk approaching her husband, the king, without him first calling for her. Fortunately for Esther, the king welcomed her; had he not done so then the statutory penalty for her boldness would have been death.

Those who have a relationship with God are invited to approach him whenever they choose to. God even encourages this – like a father wanting his children to come to him. Christians have the privilege of coming into God's presence in prayer and have an open invitation to ask him to do things for them.[2] For some people praying to God is a bit like having a wish list, but this isn't how prayer is supposed to be. It is clear from the teaching in the Bible that Christians can come to God and ask, expecting – not just wishing or hoping that he will grant their requests.[3] Coming into this relationship with God is life changing.

Pattern

The Bible is loaded with teaching about the best way to live. Probably the most well-known example of this is what is referred to as the 'sermon on the mount'.[4] The whole of the Bible is focussed on showing us the best way to live, whether by direct teaching, by illustrative stories or through what are referred to as the poetic books (for example the Old Testament book of Proverbs). Most people who have any familiarity with the Bible recognise that it has some useful teaching, but actually this teaching is far more than useful; it is life changing.[5] This is because the teaching in the Bible is based on principles that God has established. When we follow these our prospect for living successfully is dramatically enhanced.

Even for people who do not pretend to honour God or to obey him, if they follow the principles of the Bible then things go well for them. An example of this is what is known as 'servant leadership'. This is something that Jesus taught and exemplified, and that has become a mainstream leadership philosophy in business today.[6] There is recognition that when the motivation of leaders is to support and serve the people that they lead, then they are more effective leaders.

Summary

When someone becomes a Christian, it is not that this puts a gloss on their life, but rather that their life's foundations change; their life is revolutionised.

Question 66 – Am I responsible for the natural environment?

Disposability

In our kitchen we have a microwave oven that, although we had to replace a component during the earlier years of its life, has been in constant use and served us well for more than a quarter of a century. It would be good if every appliance lasted as long. Today we tend not to consider repair as an option, and don't have the expectation that our possessions will last a long time; most of us are living in a throw-away society and have a throw-away mentality. As this 'disposable' philosophy has gained momentum, there has in parallel been a growing awareness of the environmental impact of our ever-increasing consumption. This focus on the natural world is brought into particular focus when we learn of species facing extinction due to human greed – species that we may previously have taken for granted but that are now disappearing, irreplaceable, never to exist again.

Short-sightedness

In times past we have treated natural resources as something to be harvested – an infinite source that we thought of as existing for our own benefit alone. We have paid little concern to the finite nature of what we have been using up, or to the environmental impact that is so often the result of resource extraction or harvesting.

Concern for the environment isn't actually a new imperative. Implicit in the Judeo-Christian consciousness is the understanding that God created the world in which we live; essentially it is on loan to us, on trust. The environment is ours to enjoy and to cherish, but we are also to be held accountable for our stewardship of it.

Who Cares?

God created the world to sustain us both physically and aesthetically; he has made it a beautiful place to dwell. This being so, it stands to reason that God cares about the environment. He cares about how we treat it. He wants us to look after his creation, handling it with consideration and care.

Those who honour God understand their responsibility for managing the natural environment with respect. It is worth noting that the narrative at the beginning of the Bible explains that after God made the first man, Adam, he placed Adam in the Garden of Eden with instructions to tend the garden:

> *The Lord God took the man and put him in the Garden of Eden to work it and take care of it.*[1]

At first glance this appears to apply to a specific time and place, but Christians understand the instruction that God gave to the first man is equally applicable to us in the 21st century. That instruction wasn't just for there and then but was a general commission to take care of God's creation.

The greed of mankind has always been an issue. So often our approach is to take the most at the least cost to ourselves. Some may see this as a good business philosophy, but surely this is an inadequate perspective? If we see ourselves as moral beings, then we must also recognise that we have responsibilities. We have a duty to consider the impact of our actions, to clean-up after ourselves, and to harvest resources sustainably.

Facing our Responsibilities

Some, who aim to act morally within their own personal sphere, are content to acquiesce in manifestations of corporate greed. Corporations and states are sometimes in denial about their actions and fight ruthlessly for what they perceive as their own best interests, even if faced with compelling evidence that their actions are harmful. The message of the Bible is that we should each, individually, do whatever is 'right', irrespective of the cost to ourselves – to our financial wellbeing, career, or social status. We should not be allowing our morality to be dictated by anyone other than God himself and should actively seek to understand how he wants us to behave. None of us are perfect, but this only serves to emphasise our need to understand what God's will is for us.[2]

A Metaphor

So often we fail to take proper account of the implication of our actions; we do what suits us at the time, without seeing the bigger picture. The effect of our individual decisions may be unnoticeable in the short term, and yet they may be moving us inexorably towards harm. We may not recognise the damage our choices are causing until it is too late, until the damage is done. We are thinking about the natural environment here, and yet there is a clear parallel within the spiritual sphere. Many people progress through their lives with little, if any, sense of the impact of their way of life; they prefer to live in the now without considering the implications for eternity. And yet, just as the damage that we cause to the natural environment eventually catches up with us, the same is true in the spiritual realm. The message of the Bible is very clear; at the conclusion of our lives we will be required to account to God for the choices we have made, and to face the consequences.[3]

The Contract

❖ Question 67 – What qualifies me to become a Christian?

Tipping the Balance

Everyone has questions – usually quite a few! Hopefully this book has provided answers that have helped, but maybe it has not given all of the answers that you have been seeking. The bottom line is that we don't need answers to everything; we need just enough answers for the balance to be tipped, like a pair of old-fashioned weighing scales. Here it is a matter of becoming convinced about the fundamental points that were outlined in the very first topic in the Foundations section of this book – 'What is a Christian?' So here they are again, this time annotated to show why each point is important:

Qualification Requirements

- Belief in the existence of God – who is the creator and sustainer of the universe.[1]

    Christian belief is based on there being no one who is greater than God, and no one else like God; he is not one of many. He is the Creator of everything. If God is anything less than this, then he is not 'God'.

- Belief in Jesus the Son of God – that he was born and lived a life in obedience to God.[2]

    Christian belief is founded upon the person of Jesus, both who he is and how he lived. If Jesus was not a man then he was not legally qualified to stand in our place as our representative before God. If he is only a man then his sacrifice would, at best, be sufficient to cover the sins of only one human being. If Jesus was not entirely good, then he was not morally qualified to carry the burden of our wrongdoing.

- Recognition of personal failure to live the way that is pleasing to God.[3]

    We like to compare ourselves with other people; by this measure we may think that we are quite good. God doesn't do this – he compares us with himself. Using this comparison we are anything but good, and are not fit to have a relationship with God.

- Belief that Jesus died on the cross and, by doing so, took upon himself the consequences of our wrongdoing, guilt and shame.[4]

    Someone had to take our place in paying our debts which we cannot pay off ourselves. Jesus did this – he had no guilt of his own but paid the price (death) of the guilty (us). Instead of carrying any guilt of his own, he carried ours, dying in our place. When Jesus, who is himself God, died in our place he carried the sin of the whole world.

- Recognition that God offers forgiveness and a new life to anyone who asks to be reconciled to him, based on the work done by Jesus when he died in our place.[5]

    We can now come to God and ask to be reconciled to him, not because we are good enough, but because Jesus is. Jesus carried our sin and took our punishment upon himself. So when we ask this of God, the punishment that we are due has already been paid – God can forgive us and accept us into a close relationship with himself.

God is not an Amorphous Blob

Some time ago I taught a series in my church on the subject of the Trinity (see the Study Room – Q 9). In the first sermon I outlined the importance of the Trinity as foundational Christian teaching and, totally unscripted, made the statement that "God is not an amorphous blob." The point I was making was that although we cannot hope to fathom the depths of who God is, we are able to know, and to some extent appreciate, certain things about God – his triune (three in unity) nature being one of these.

Good Enough

The question we are considering now refers to being 'qualified' to become a Christian. The use of this term will alarm some people, but just as there are things that we can know, and need to know, about the nature of God, so we need a basis of understanding upon which to act if we are to be reconciled to God. Just as God is not an 'amorphous blob', so the exercise of faith is not based on something vague and uncertain.

The use of the term 'qualified' in the present topic is not to suggest that we need to be good enough, because there is nothing that we can ever hope to do to make ourselves good enough to be in relationship with God. In fact, our 'qualification' for reconciliation with God is based on an appreciation of who and what we are: our frailty, failure and sin. Just as when we die we leave everything behind, so we can only come to God in this life 'empty-handed', casting ourselves upon his mercy.

From the perspective of 'qualification', being convinced about the five points outlined above, qualifies you to approach God and ask to be reconciled to him.

❖ **Question 68 – What does it mean to become a Christian?**

A False Assumption

Nothing in my previous experience had indicated that being 'religious' and a church goer didn't make me a Christian, but at the age of seventeen I was confronted with the stark fact that it did not; I was not. This happened late one afternoon at a college Christian Union meeting when the speaker explained what it meant to be a Christian. Afterwards, while waiting for the bus that would take me home, a friend who had also been at the meeting stated that if what we had heard was true then he himself wasn't a Christian. In my heart I knew that the same applied to me; the bottom line was that I didn't actually have a relationship with God.

Facing the Truth

This was decision time for me; my choice was between pretending that all was well and carrying on regardless of what I now knew or facing the truth and doing something about it. I saw my situation pictorially. Some way behind me there had been a junction in the path, a crossroads, where I needed to have turned but had carried straight on.[1] I could decide to continue forward now, but knew that to do this and still pretend that I was a Christian would be fraudulent. The alternative was to retrace my steps back to the junction and decide to take the path that meant having a relationship with God.[2] I weighed this up very carefully.

Double-sided Coin

From the way that it had been explained to me, I recognised that there were two aspects to becoming a Christian, like two sides of a coin. The face of the coin represented being forgiven for the wrongs that I had done and being reconciled to God, coming into relationship with him based on his love for me. On the reverse side of the coin was living my life the way God wants, trusting him and being submitted to his will and purpose for my life.[3]

The Reverse

I thought a lot about the reverse side of the coin. In effect this involved handing over the direction of my life to God. It seemed reasonable that if God loved me (and I had come to believe that he did), and if he had a plan and a purpose for my life (and I was persuaded that he had), that I could trust him in this. In fact, if these things were true, then my choice was between stumbling along on my own or following the perfect plan of a loving heavenly father (God). I thought about what I considered to be the three big decisions that I might face, and whether I was prepared to seek God's direction in these; would I be prepared to follow whatever way he led me. These were the three specific things that I weighed up:

- Career – was I prepared to follow God's plan for my working life rather than do what seemed best to me? I decided that he knew best and that to follow his direction in this would be a sound strategy.

- Marriage – was I prepared to marry the person he showed me, rather than choose whoever took my fancy? I realised that this hugely important decision was best made with the guidance of God who knows me better than anybody.

- Calling – what if God were to ask me to work for him in some remote and distant part of the world - would I be prepared to do this? I realised that if God loves me and has the best possible plan for my life, then even if this meant doing something that would seem extreme to me, then this must be the situation where he would bless me, and I would be most fulfilled.

Choosing

The outcome was that I decided that I believed in God, believed that he truly loved me, and believed that Jesus had died in my place. I also decided that if God had a plan for my life then it would be very unwise to disregard it and continue to go my own way.

To summarise the answer to the current question: to become a Christian means to receive God's forgiveness for your sin, and to invite Jesus to be in charge of your life.

By the way, while it was right to weigh up whether I was willing to do whatever God asked of me, no matter how extreme this might appear, most people discover that God asks them to do things that are much more 'normal' (as has been my experience). He mostly asks us to serve him in our own culture and environment.

❖ Question 69 – How do I become a Christian?

One Final Obstacle

Assuming that you have carefully considered the previous two questions, there might still be one obstacle. Some people come to a place of being convinced; they understand about God's forgiveness and are willing for Jesus to be in charge of their live – but a fundamental problem still remains.

Some people struggle with the fact that reconciliation with God is a free gift.[1] They would like to receive this, but not as a gift. They want to be able in some way to earn or deserve what God is offering. Some people say that they 'don't accept charity' – the problem here is that this literally is 'charity' and is the only way that reconciliation with God is possible.

Empty-Handed

Jesus paid the price of our wrongdoing when he died on the cross – he did this for a simple reason – because we are not capable of doing it ourselves. Why is this? It is because of the state that we are in. We can see this described in the Old Testament book of Isaiah where we read:

> We are all infected and impure with sin. When we put on our prized robes of righteousness, we find they are but filthy rags.[2]

The bottom line is that we have nothing that we can bring to God as a basis for him to forgive us. This is why God himself had to provide a means for us to be forgiven – Jesus.

Undeserved

There was a time when I felt desperate to hear from God, but he was silent. I wanted guidance, but God wanted me to trust him and to be patient. If God had told me to walk from John O' Groats in the very north of Scotland, to Land's End at the most southerly point on mainland Britain, and that once I had done so I would hear from him, then I would have grabbed my backpack in an instant. But with God we cannot earn anything; everything is provided by his loving kindness, not because we deserve it. I hope that this isn't a problem for you, but if it is then you will not be able to move on spiritually until you lay down your pride and accept that God's forgiveness is a gift that neither you nor anyone else can ever earn or deserve.

It Couldn't be Easier

Once you have weighed everything and decided that you want to live your life on God's terms, actually becoming a Christian couldn't be easier - all you need do is to ask him. You can ask him anywhere and at any time – but you have to do this yourself, in your own heart; others can't do it for you. You can use your own words, but if you struggle to know what to say then here is an example prayer that you could use:

> "Heavenly Father, I have lived my life in ways that haven't pleased you; I am sorry and I ask you to forgive me for all my failings, because Jesus died in my place.
>
> Jesus, I invite you to be Lord of my life. From now on I want to live the way that you will show me; I ask you to lead me into a new way of living that is pleasing to you."

Everything Changes

If you have prayed a prayer like this with an honest heart, then you have made a transaction with God and he will have fulfilled his part.[3] You may experience a freedom in your spirit, but however you feel, things have changed – you are now a Christian. You are now able to live a new life in relationship with the Living God.

Question 70 – Now that I am a Christian – what next?

New Home

Becoming a Christian is like signing the contract and completing the transaction to buy the house – it is now your house, your future home.[1] You now look forward to occupying the house, discovering all of the different spaces and features, and enjoying living in your new home. When moving to a new house we all need help to actually move in, whether from friends, family or a removals company, maybe all three. In the case of moving into our spiritual new home this help may come from individual Christian friends or family members who are Christians, but it also comes from the church. The church is God's 'big idea' for helping each of us to understand his ways and to provide an environment that supports spiritual growth and development.[2]

Help is at Hand

You may already know some Christians, or even have links to a church. On the other hand you might have read this book without being aware that anyone you know is a Christian. The important thing now is for you to avoid trying to 'go it alone'. You have a new relationship with God, but part of his plan for you is that you are also built into his church, that you become part of the church (see the Dining Room section of this book).

Where to Belong

Taking this on board, one of the first things to ask in prayer to God is that he guides you to a church that will be a help to you on your continuing spiritual journey. If you already have Christian friends then it may seem right to join with their church, but don't assume this; God may have other plans. If you bring this need to God in prayer, then he will guide you – don't be afraid to keep reminding him until you are confident that you have the guidance that you need. When you do find a church that you believe is the right place to settle, talk to the leaders about the spiritual journey that you have come on and share how you became a Christian. They will be thrilled to hear your story and will know how to help you on your adventure with God.

The Book

Another important 'next step' is to begin to read the Bible (see the Foundations section – Q 4).[3] If you don't already have a modern translation of the Bible, then try to obtain one – the important thing is to have a copy of the Bible that is in clear English (not one that uses outdated language). If you have Christian friends then they can advise you about what version it would be good to get. Personally, I use the New International Version, and can recommend this; it is easy to read and a sound translation of the original languages.

Once you have a Bible, the next thing to consider is where to start reading. A good place would be one of the four gospel accounts at the beginning of the New Testament. It doesn't matter which one you choose; however, the Gospel according to John is often suggested. You might then move on to reading the next book which is the Acts of the Apostles.

Talking and Listening

The third and most important thing that you will want to do as a new Christian is to become accustomed to praying. This is how we communicate with God, whether asking him about things, or receiving guidance from him, or just being still in his presence.[4] Prayer is not like using the telephone – it costs nothing and God doesn't mind when, how often or for how long we speak to him. In fact, God loves to hear from us and is delighted whenever we turn aside to spend time with him.

POSTSCRIPT

Well this is it. You have read the book and here you are at the end – almost. Wherever you started from, I hope that you can appreciate the importance of what you have been reading – you might think of it as a manifesto for God's kingdom and your own life. If you are not a Christian already, then you are faced with a decision – one that you are now equipped to make. This is absolutely the most important decision that you have ever made or will ever make.

Once we have viewed a house that is on the market, we need to decide quickly whether we want it or not, otherwise someone else may jump in ahead of us. You are not in a competition in the same way here, but the choice is similar. If you sense that God loves you, has a plan for you, and wants a relationship with you, then you can snub him if you want to. But if your heart is set on responding and accepting his offer of forgiveness and a new life, then respond now – don't keep him waiting. The house is ready for you to move into. God offers you a clean slate, a fresh start, a new direction, hope for the future – choose the new life that is on offer through Jesus.

In one sense the concept of *The Viewing* is back to front. There is a verse in the last book of the Bible which uses a similar analogy to a house, but here Jesus is on the outside of the house and is knocking at the door, asking to be let in. The house that he wants to come into is your life. Will you open the door to him; will you allow him in?

I leave you with my very best wishes for your future,

John

For more information, or to leave a book review, visit the author's website at:
www.askedquestions.org

REFERENCE INDEX

Finding your way in the Bible

Bible references follow a standard convention as:

      John 3:16   = the Bible book or letter (John)

      John **3**:16   = the chapter in the book (3)

      John 3:**16**   = the verse in the chapter (16)

Sometimes there are several verses, shown as:

      16-18   = three verses in a row

      16, 19   = two separate verses in the same chapter

      16-18, 19   = three verses followed by one other

      John 3:16; Romans 5:8 = two separate verses/passages

Sometimes references refer to a part of a verse. These show either **a** or **b** after the verse to indicate the first half or the second, as in Acts 1:4**b**.

If you don't have a copy of the Bible in modern English, and want to check out some of the references, then you can use an online Bible such as www.biblegateway.com. Here you can choose from many different translations or versions.

Except where stated otherwise, the Bible references listed below are to the New International Version (2011)

    Bible Gateway: "New International Version – UK (NIVUK)".

Other Bible references are to The Living Bible (1971)

    Bible Gateway: "Living Bible (TLB)".

ENDNOTES

The Foundations

Question 1

1) Hebrews 11:7

2) Isaiah 42:5; Jeremiah 32:17

3) Philippians 2:5-8

4) Romans 3:23, 1 John 1:8

5) 1 Peter 2:24

6) John 3:16; Acts 13:38,39

7) Hebrews 11:6

Question 2

1) 1 Timothy 2:5

2) Exodus 3:14

3) Romans 1:20

Question 3
1) Philippians 2:13

Question 4

1) Matthew 3:17

2) Matthew 1:1; 1:18

3) Hebrews 4:12

Question 5

1) John 18:38

2) John 8:32

3) Matthew 7:8

The Study

Question 6

1) Exodus 3:1-4

2) Genesis chapters 6-8

3) Jonah (the book)

Question 7

1) Genesis 1:28

2) Fazale Runa & Hugh Ross. *Origins of Life*, Navpress, 2004.

Question 8

1) Micah 5:2; Isaiah 7:14; 9:6,7

2) Luke 1:35

3) Luke 2:26-35

4) Matthew 19:28; Revelation 7:15-17

5) Romans 5:6-8

6) Luke 24:7

7) Acts 1:9-11

Question 9

1) 2 Corinthians 5:14

2) Genesis 1:26

3) Isaiah 9:6

4) Mark 1:11

5) John 1:1

6) John 1:18

7) Mark 12:29

8) 1 Corinthians 8:4

Question 10

1) 1 Timothy 1:3; 2 Peter 2:1; 2 John:7

Question 11

1) Numbers 23:19

2) 1 Samuel 15:29

Question 12

1) 1 John 4:8

2) W.E. Vine. *Expository Dictionary of Bible Words*, HarperCollins, 1981.

The Lounge

Question 13

1) Genesis 28:3, 35:11, 49:25 – God Almighty (El Shaddai)

2) Genesis 2:19-24

3) Galatians 3:26-29

4) Ephesians 5:24,25

Question 14

1) John 14:6

2) John 3:34-36

Question 15

1) 1 Timothy 2:5

2) Deuteronomy 9:7-8, 12, 15-16

3) John 14:6; Acts 4:12

4) Isaiah 53 (Full chapter)

5) Isaiah 49:6; Luke 2:30-32

Question 16

1) Titus 1:15,16

2) 1 Timothy 6:3-5

3) Galatians 5:1-6

4) 1 Timothy 2:5

Question 17

1) Acts 7:39-41

2) John 14:6; Acts 4:12; 1 Timothy 2:5,6

Question 18

1) Genesis 2:15-17

2) Genesis 3:7

3) Genesis 3:16-19

4) Proverbs 3:12; Hebrews 12:6

5) Proverbs 13:24 (The Living Bible)

6) 1 John 1:5-10

7) Ecclesiastes 7:20

Question 20

1) 1 Corinthians 4:20; 2 Corinthians 10:4

Question 21

1) Acts 9:1-6

Question 22

1) Romans 16:17

Question 23

1) 1 Samuel 16:7

2) 2 Corinthians 5:20; Eph 6:20

3) Romans 12:2

Question 24

1) 2 Kings 7:1-11

2) Mark 16:15,16; Acts 1:8

The Television Room

Question 25

1) Genesis 2:15

2) Genesis 3:17-19

3) Mathew 19:28; 1 Corinthians 6:3; Revelation 3:21; 2 Timothy 2:11-13; Revelation 22:3-5

4) 2 Peter 3:10; Matt 24:35

5) John 12:48-50

Question 26

1) Ephesians 6:12

2) 2 Timothy 2:26

3) 2 Corinthians 2:11; John

8:44; Ephesians 6:11; 1
Peter 5:8

4) Colossians 2:15

5) Matthew 25:41;
Revelation 20:10

Question 27

1) Matthew 13:19 & 38

2) 2 Corinthians 11:14;
Ezekiel 28:14,15

3) Ephesians 6:12

4) Psalm 14:1

5) Romans 3:23

Question 28

1) Luke 16:19-30

2) Matthew 12:36,37

3) Revelation 16:7

4) Psalm 143:2

5) 2 Corinthians 5:10

Question 29

1) John 15:26

2) John 14:26

3) Acts 1:8

4) 1 Corinthians 12:8-10

5) 1 Corinthians 12:11;
Romans 12:6,7

Question 30

1) Matthew 4:23; 9:35

2) Acts 3

3) Acts 4:13

4) Matthew 10:8

5) 1 Corinthians 12:9

Question 31

1) Psalm 103:12 (The Living
Bible)

2) Isaiah 1:18

3) Hebrews 4:12

4) Matthew 23:27,28

5) Romans 12:2

Question 32

1) 1 Kings 19:11,12

2) Hebrews 11:6; Matthew
7:7,8

Question 33

1) John 14:3

2) Acts 1:9-11

3) Matthew 24:36-39

4) Mark 13:26,27; 1 Thessalonians 4:15-17; Hebrews 9:27,28

The Kitchen

Question 34

1) Deuteronomy 5:22

2) Deuteronomy 4:13

3) Exodus 20:3-17

4) Matthew 5:19

5) Galatians 3:11; Proverbs 3:5,6

Question 35

1) Matthew 23:3,4

2) Romans 14:14,15

Question 36

1) Exodus 23:23-33

2) Jeremiah 31:30 – see also Ezekiel 18

Question 37

1) James 2:17; 2:26

2) James 2:8

3) Luke 10:27

4) Romans 12:2

5) Luke 10:30-37

6) Acts 3:1-10

Question 38

1) John 14:23,24a

2) Romans 7:14,15, 21-25

3) Romans 8:7

4) Romans 12:2

Question 39

1) Hebrews 13:17

2) James 3:1

3) Ephesians 5:21

4) Colossians 3:15-17

5) 1 Corinthians 14:26

Question 40

1) Romans 6:1-5

2) Galatians 5:1

3) Ephesians 4:22-24

4) 2 Timothy 1:9; 2 Peter 1:2-4 – see The Living Bible

The Dining Room

Question 41

1) 1 Timothy 3:15

2) Acts 14:27

3) Colossians 4:15

4) 1 Corinthians 1:2

5) 1 Corinthians 12:12-27

6) 1 Corinthians 12:4-6

Question 42

1) Hebrews 10:24,25

2) Acts 2:46,47

3) 1 Thessalonians 5:11

4) Romans 8:7,8

5) 1 John 4:20,21

6) Hebrews 13:17

7) Matthew 18:21,22

8) Matthew 6:12

Question 43

1) 1 Timothy 6:10

2) Matthew 6:21

3) 2 Corinthians 9:6,7

Question 44

1) Hebrews 12:28,29

2) Hebrews 10:24,25

3) 2 Corinthians 11:13

4) 2 Peter 2:1

5) James 1:5-8

Question 45

1) Acts 8:25; 40

2) Matthew 7:7,8

3) 2 Timothy 2:2; Mark 16:15

Question 46

1) Acts 11:15

2) Acts 1:4b,5

3) Acts 2:1-12

4) Acts 10:44-47

The Bathroom

Question 47

1) Ecclesiastes 7:20

2) Psalm 103:11,12

3) Romans 3:23

4) Genesis 1:28

5) Psalm 14:3

6) 1 Samuel 16:7

7) Matthew 5:28

Question 48

1) Luke 4:18

2) Galatians 5:1

3) Hebrews 9:14

4) Psalm 34:5 – see the New Living Translation

Question 49

1) Romans 3:10,11

2) Romans 2:15; 2 Samuel 24:10

Question 50

1) Psalm 139:1-4

2) Psalm 44:20,21

3) Isaiah 55:8,9

4) Genesis 1:27

5) Ephesians 1:4-6

6) Mark 1:11; Luke 9:35

7) 1 Peter 1:20

8) Isaiah 1:18

9) Isaiah 53:5

10) Ephesians 2:1-5

Question 51

1) Genesis 2:15-17

2) Genesis 3:1-5

3) Genesis 3:8,9

4) Romans 3:23

5) 1 Corinthians 15:21-23

Question 52

1) Ephesians 6:20

2) Hebrews 13:21; Jeremiah 29:11

Question 53

1) 1 John 1:8,9

2) Matthew 27:46

3) 1 Corinthians 15:3; Colossians 3:13

4) Luke 6:37,38

The Bedroom

Question 54

1) Genesis 2:18

2) Isaiah 42:6,7

3) Ephesians 5:31,32

4) Genesis 9:11

5) Genesis 9:16

6) Ephesians 2:14-18

7) Ephesians 5:25-27; 2 Corinthians 11:2

8) Matthew 19:4-6

9) Mark 16:16

10) Colossians 2:12; 1 Peter 3:21

Question 55

1) 1 Peter 4:3; Ephesians 2:1-3; Romans 13:13

2) 2 Corinthians 5:20

3) 2 Timothy 2:24-26

4) 1 Corinthians 6:9-11

Question 56

1) Genesis 2:24

2) Colossians 3:5; Ephesians 5:3; Hebrews 13:4

Question 57

1) Leviticus 18:22; Leviticus 20:13; Romans 1:24; Romans 1:26-27; 1 Timothy 1:8-11

2) Genesis 2:23,24

3) 1 Thessalonians 4:3-6

4) 1 John 1:5-10; Romans 3:22-26

5) 1 Corinthians 6:9-11

6) Isaiah 5:20

Question 58

1) Genesis 1:27,28

2) Deuteronomy 22:5

3) Isaiah 56:4,5

4) Acts 13:38-39

Question 59

1) 1 Corinthians 5:13

2) Hebrews 4:15

3) 2 Corinthians 11:29

4) 2 Timothy 1:7

5) 1 Timothy 3:2-12; Titus 1:6-9

6) 1 Corinthians 7:5-9

Question 60

1) 1 Corinthians 7:32-35

2) Romans 14:10-12

3) Proverbs 3:5,6

4) Acts 11:25 onwards

The Roof

Question 61

1) Genesis 2:8,9; Isaiah 51:3

2) Genesis 3:23

3) Romans 8:3

4) Romans 8:32

5) Job 1:11

6) Job 2:5

7) Job 13:15

8) Jonah 1:17

Question 62

1) John 11:35

2) John 11:38

3) 1 John 2:2 (The Living Bible)

4) Matthew 27:46, Mark 15:34

5) Revelation 21:4

The Garden

Question 63

1) Ecclesiastes 1:9

2) Matthew 6:27

3) Matthew 6:34

4) John 3:16

5) Jeremiah 29:11

6) Philippians 2:13; 2 Timothy 1:9

7) Romans 8:16

Question 64

1) Psalm 144:3,4

2) Romans 8:28

3) Acts 3:19

Question 65

1) Esther 4:11

2) Matthew 7:8; John 16:24

3) Ephesians 3:20; James 1:6-8

4) Matthew 5:1

5) Psalm 119:105; 129,130

6) Mark 9:35

Question 66

1) Genesis 2:15

2) Romans 12:2

3) 2 Corinthians 5:10

The Contract

Question 67

1) Isaiah 42:5; Jeremiah 32:17

2) Philippians 2:5-8

3) Romans 3:23, 1 John 1:8

4) 1 Peter 2:24; 1 John 2:2

5) John 3:16; Acts 13:38,39

Question 68

1) Jeremiah 6:16

2) Matthew 7:13,14

3) James 4:7-10

Question 69

1) Romans 6:23; Revelation 22:17

2) Isaiah 64:6 (The Living Bible)

3) Luke 11:10; Revelation 3:20

Question 70

1) 2 Corinthians 6:1,2

2) Colossians 3:16; 1 Thessalonians 5:11; Hebrews 10:24,25

3) 2 Timothy 3:16

4) Philippians 4:6; Romans 12:12